John Adams Allen

Medical Examinations for life Insurance

John Adams Allen

Medical Examinations for life Insurance

ISBN/EAN: 9783743330221

Manufactured in Europe, USA, Canada, Australia, Japa

Cover: Foto ©ninafisch / pixelio.de

Manufactured and distributed by brebook publishing software (www.brebook.com)

John Adams Allen

Medical Examinations for life Insurance

MEDICAL EXAMINATIONS

FOR

LIFE INSURANCE.

BY

J. ADAMS ALLEN, M.D. LL. D.,

PROF. PRINCIPLES AND PRACTICE OF MEDICINE AND CLINICAL MEDICINE IN RUSH MEDICAL COLLEGE; FORMERLY
PROF. PHYSIOLOGY AND PATHOLOGY IN THE UNIVERSITY OF MICHIGAN.

EIGHTH EDITION:
REVISED AND ENLARGED,
With new Introductory Chapter and an Extensive Appendix.

NEW YORK AND CHICAGO
THE SPECTATOR COMPANY,
PUBLISHERS,
1886.

Entered according to Act of Congress, in the year 1880,

By THE SPECTATOR COMPANY,

In the office of the Librarian of Congress, Washington, D. C.

THE SPECTATOR PRESS,
No. 16 Dey Street, New York.

Preface to Eighth Edition.

The exhaustion of six editions of this brief manual within a few months, sufficiently demonstrates the want which has been felt for some work of the character. The Author tenders his sincere acknowledgements for the kindly terms in which many of the most distinguished Medical Examiners throughout the country have been pleased to welcome its publication. He is fully sensible of the difficulties necessarily incident to the effort to take an intermediate course between the voluminous and elaborate treatise and the mere tractate. This little book is published as a chart, and not as an exhaustive volume.

The effort has been to bring fairly before the Medical Examiner the salient points of his business, in as concise a form as perspicuity would possibly permit.

In the present edition there has been but little change, save in the addition of an Appendix containing matter, which, it is believed, will add considerably to the value of the work, and also an Introductory Chapter, calling the especial attention of Examiners to the importance of the relations they sustain to their respective Companies; to the parties examined, and to the profession.

Attention is called to the Index of the Appendix, on page 169, which indicates the general character of the additions made. The contained tables are believed to be valuable.

In the preparation of these additions, the Author begs leave to acknowledge the important services of I. N. DANFORTH, M. D., of this city—not only a medical examiner of large experience, but an accomplished professional scholar and writer.

Under the pressure of his own multitudinous affairs, the Author has delayed publication of a new edition until the previous one was long out of print. Advantage has been taken of this delay to seek for the opinions and suggestions of professional Life Insurance men, both lay and professional. These have been regarded in this edition, so far as they have appeared correct and feasible.

In order not to make the volume too bulky, the Appendix and Introductory chapters have been given in smaller type than used in the text.

J. A. A.

INTRODUCTION.

It is now about one hundred and fifty years since life insurance first established itself on anything like an enduring basis. Commencing with the "Amicable Society," of London, it has steadily grown in public favor until, at the present day, no form of investment is regarded with greater favor, by even the shrewdest and most sagacious business men, than the stocks of life insurance companies, and policies of insurance on their own lives. At every step of its progress, this noble institution has sought the aid and counsel of the medical profession. It has its very basis and foundation, in fact, in the established laws of mortality, as carefully and patiently worked out by medical men. The first life company was only started after Dr. Halley, of London, had made that series of observations regarding the duration of human life, out of which grew the "Breslau table of mortality." Every important step in life insurance has been preceded by a pioneer corps of physicians, who have carefully marked out the way; and, in no single instance, has future experience proved the falsity or unreliability of their conclusions.

If all this be true, it follows that the relations of the medical profession to the interests of life insurance are vastly important; and that they are certainly quite as important to the insured party, as to the company insuring. For our present purposes, it will be convenient to consider the relations of Medical Examiners to life insurance, and the insurance interests, under three heads, to-wit: Their relations to life companies employing them, or to the companies' agents. Secondly, to applicants, or parties seeking insurance; and thirdly, to the medical profession.

First: their relations to companies, or agents of companies. It is scarcely too much to say that the ultimate safety and stability of every life insurance company rests in the hands of those who decide upon the character of its risks: for, however great may be its resources, or with however much of financial skill and sagacity its affairs may be managed, or however many or perfect may be its "tables of mortality," it is absolutely certain to come to a disastrous end, unless its risks are selected with care and discrimination. And so many, and so insidious are the diseases whereof the end is only too certainly fatal, that this can only be done by the skilled and experienced Physician. To render the office of Medical Examiner to the greatest degree useful, three things seem to the writer absolutely essential: (1st) That the best talent be secured. (2d) That perfect harmony be maintained between the Examiner and the company's representative or agent. (3d) That the Examiner be appointed from the central office: that he be recognized as an officer *de facto* of the company, independent, and therefore self-reliant, in his sphere; and responsible for the proper management of the interests committed to his charge.

(1st) It is an absolute and palpable *wrong* for any company to appoint as its Examiners men deficient in knowledge; in high-toned honesty, in devotion to the interests of their profession, or men who are wanting in that practical wisdom which can only be acquired by actual experience. It is wrong, in that it must, to a greater or less extent, militate against, rather than contribute to, the safety of the company; it is wrong, in that it needlessly places in jeopardy the interests of those who are entirely unable to protect themselves, namely, the policyholders, or those who are dependent upon them; and lastly, it is wrong, in that it must inevitably bring undeserved odium and disgrace upon the medical profession. Notwithstanding the hordes of quacks and charlatans which infest every community, competent and faithful Medical Examiners can almost everywhere be found; but while the former are forever *seeking* appointments, the latter must generally be *sought*; the former are only too apt to foist their services upon the unwary agent;

the latter very properly regard their services as worth *seeking*, if worth *having*. Every company ought to be held to a stern and rigid accountability for the character and ability of its Examiners; it is the custodian of vastly important interests, which, from the very nature of the case, cannot be looked after by those most interested in its integrity. Its policyholders are scattered over every State in the Union, and they, as well as the Examiners upon whose recommendation they are accepted, must of necessity be entire strangers to the Managers and Consulting Physician. But these facts furnish not the least excuse for appointing —or at all events, for *retaining* incompetent Examiners; rather do they render it more imperatively the duty of those selecting them, to exercise the greatest care in obtaining honest and skilled physicians to fulfill this most important trust; and, so perfect and complete are the means for acquiring information at the present day, that no company can plead ignorance regarding the qualifications of its Examiners, and at the same time, maintain a creditable reputation for shrewdness and good management.

(2d.) Unless perfect harmony be maintained between the Examiner and the Agent under whom he is acting, the company's interests must necessarily suffer. The former is not unfrequently *compelled* to reject risks upon which the latter has expended no inconsiderable amount of time and labor, and which, in case of rejection, must go for nothing. Moreover, applicants are often rejected for reasons which are only apparent to the Examiner; and, to the uneducated ear, or unskilled touch of the Agent, this seems an unwarranted stretch of power on the part of the former. With the Agent it is a question of *commissions;* with the Examiner it is a question of *safety;* and these two interests sometimes stand diametrically opposed to each other. But it is for precisely this reason that the Medical Examiner is employed at all; and, unless he resolutely stands, like an alert and faithful sentinel, between the company on the one hand, and the unsafe and undesirable applicant seeking admission thereto on the other, he signally fails of fulfilling his obligations to the former, and renders his office not only useless, but positively harmful. This course, however, although exceedingly desirable and important so far as the *company* is concerned, must of course sometimes array him in direct opposition to the pecuniary interests of the Agent. But with this the Examiner must and can have nothing to do; it is no concern of his whether the Agent is remunerated by stated commissions or a regular salary: he has only to do with the safety or unsafety of the risk; and, while he must disregard all else but this, he must, at the same time, maintain harmonious relations with the Agent. We propose to indicate, in the next place, how, in our judgment, this can best be done.

(3d.) The Medical Examiner, at least in every situation involving any considerable number of examinations, and especially in the large cities and populous towns, where almost every applicant is more than likely to be an absolute stranger to both Agent and Examiner, should be appointed by the authorities at the home office, after they shall have satisfied themselves that he is precisely the man for the place, and unless they are well convinced of this, he should be dismissed and another and more satisfactory appointment should be made. Whatever may be the actual merit of the Examiner, unless he is fortunate enough to possess the entire confidence of the Managers—especially the Consulting Physician—at the central office, he cannot resign too soon. For, unless the central authorities implicitly confide in him, it will be impossible for the Local Agent to respect either him or his decisions in regard to applicants—especially if they happen, as they sometimes must, to be adverse to the interests of the Agent. For this reason the Examiner should stand in the attitude of an officer, recognized as such by the company; his department should stand by itself, subject only to the control of, and responsible only to, the home office. He should not be a mere "tenant at will," subject to ejectment at the pleasure or caprice of the Agent; for such an equivocal position would be derogatory, not to the *man* only, but to the position he vainly attempted to fill. The general adoption of this course on the part of the companies, will most certainly enable them to secure and permanently retain the best medical talent, and also insure harmonious action between the Agent and Examiner—both of which conditions are exceedingly important and desirable.

Secondly: The relations of Examiners to parties seeking assurance. The Examiner is of course bound to consider the interests of the company by whom he is employed and paid, as paramount to all others;

else would he absolutely endanger, rather than contribute to the company's safety and stability. But while this is undeniably true, it is also true that the applicant has claims which he cannot properly disregard. Life insurance has now become something more than a mere *privilege;* it has come to be almost a sacred and "inalienable" *right* to every person who is eligible thereto: and no applicant should be lightly or needlessly rejected. Every applicant coming before the Examiner is entitled to a fair and impartial examination; if obscure or unusual symptoms present themselves, he is fairly entitled to a second examination, or even more than that if necessary to a proper understanding of the case. Frequently does it happen that some apparently grave symptoms depends upon a merely temporary cause; for example, applicants in perfect health sometimes present themselves with an unusually rapid pulse, or with the respiration unaccountably frequent, or with countenance flushed and excited—and all this may be the consequence of excitement or perhaps fear; for, to very many people, a Physician's office is as terrible as the dungeons of the Inquisition; and the *very best* insurance risks are those which are least familiar with the sanctums of Doctors, and therefore most likely to give full scope to their imaginations. Individual peculiarities or "idiosyncracies" are sometimes met with, which, though generally indicative of some grave and perhaps incurable disease, are quite normal as regards the persons presenting them; these exceptional cases demand a fair hearing at the hands of the Examiner; though it must be admitted, as a general rule, that absolute strangers, presenting symptoms which are ordinarily associated with organic disease of any important organ, must be rejected, even though they may be in other respects desirable.

In making examinations preliminary to life insurance as well as in all other investigations of this character, the Physician is likely to become acquainted with matters of a strictly confidential nature, which if divulged, might prove seriously detrimental to the party. The same standard of high-toned professional honor should guide the Examiner in his relations to applicants for life insurance, as he feels constantly bound to observe in his relations to patients under his care; no excuse can be found for disregarding this matter in the one case, that will not apply with equal force to the other, except, of course, that the Examiner is bound to disclose to the Consulting Physician all facts *essential* to a correct understanding of the case. Finally, the Examiner should not forget that, however unimportant it may be to him, individually, whether an applicant be accepted or rejected, it may be and often is a matter of vast importance to the latter. Many a man turns to life insurance as the only means by which he can provide for the necessities of those he expects to leave behind him, when he shall have passed away; many an unfortunate man, whose life may have been one constant struggle with adversity, sees in a policy of insurance the only means by which he can protect his family from actual want, after he has ceased to live. Such cases must not be lightly rejected; they are always entitled to a careful and candid examination, made under circumstances which are not unfavorable to the applicant; symptoms which are merely the result of trepidation or of the excitement of the occasion, should be cleared up, and, in all regards, the Examiner should give the applicant a fair and impartial hearing, with the fixed resolution of rendering a decision which shall be just to both parties; and while this rule applies with peculiar force to the class of cases just cited, *every* applicant, whether high or low, rich or poor, fortunate or unfortunate, has the unquestionable right to expect precisely the same kind of treatment; and, when it is added that a needless rejection is a permanent and irreparable injury, inasmuch as it must always stand as a grave objection—perhaps an insuperable bar—to the acceptance of the rejected party by other companies, it will be seen that these observations are based upon principles which cannot be lightly disregarded, without doing violence to the demands of justice and equity.

Thirdly: the relations of the examiner to the Medical Profession. Every Medical Examiner is, in an important sense, a "representative man," to the company employing him, as well as to parties seeking insurance. He is to them the exponent of the present standard of medical excellence; for, it cannot reasonably be supposed that a powerful corporation would deliberately appoint, or, at all events, long retain, as the custodians of its safety, inferior or incompetent men, when the best talent is quite as easily accessible, and involves no greater outlay of expense. Let no Medical Examiner for a moment suppose that he has a merely *personal* interest in acquitting himself creditably and honorably; that his *individual* interests are *alone* to suffer if he fails to perform his duties satisfactorily; but let him always remember that he has been selected on acccount of his presumed ability and acquirements; that every blunder he commits, and every unprofessional or undignified act he allows himself to perform reflects with damaging force not on himself only, but on the Profession as a whole. It is just as imperatively his duty to maintain a high standard of professional honor in the discharge of his duties as Examiner for an insurance company, as it is in any other duty connected with his vocation; just as much his duty to examine an applicant carefully, as to diagnosticate a case he proposes to treat carefully; just as much his duty to frown upon and discountenance quackery and charlatanism in this matter as in any other. And this is due to the insurance companies, no less than to the medical profession; ever since its origin, the interests of life insurance have been, to a great extent, committed to the hands of Physicians, and, from the very nature of the case, this state of things must continue; they alone are capable of deciding as to the safety or unsafety of risks, and they alone are capable of making the observations necessary to a correct understanding of the laws of mortality. But in still another and no less important direction do the investigations of medical men subserve the interests of life insurance, namely, in observing the laws and conditions of health, and disseminating information thereupon among the people; in arresting the progress of contagious diseases, and rendering them comparatively harmless, and in enforcing salutary regulations for the preservation of the public health in cities and towns. The tendency of all this is to enhance the value of human life; to render the business of life insurance less hazardous, and therfore to bring it more directly within reach of those most likely to be benefited thereby; thus making it not only theoretically, but really, a boon and a blessing to those who are unable to make any other provision for the prospective necessities of their famlies. To such a work as this, the medical profession ought to yield an active and hearty support, not only in the persons of a few of its members, but as a compact and united whole. To this end let Medical Examiners so discharge their duties as to increase the confidence of the companies in the profession; let them remember that, to the companies, they are the acknowledged exponents of the standard of professional acquirement, honor and integrity, and let them remember that *they* have *their* part to perform towards making life insurance, in a larger sense, the institution of the people.

Note Prefatory.

Life Insurance is rapidly growing in public favor, and it is not extravagant to say that the time is coming when it will be more general even than Fire Insurance. All men have lives — not all have houses, stores, or barns. The system of endowments, non-forfeiting policies, etc., has gone far toward making what before was considered extra-prudential and exceptional, a matter of ordinary business caution and common usage. That the Insurance Companies and the holders of their policies should have the highest possible advantage, it is clearly necessary that none but lives selected with great care should be assured. Hence the MEDICAL EXAMINER becomes their indispensable agent. To aid him in the performance of his important work, is the object of this little Manual.

It is not its intention to be argumentative, statistical, or rhetorical. Neither originality in substance nor method is sought after—but only that more clearness, definiteness, and certainty may be achieved, by attention to the suggestions herein contained.

A prime object has been to concentrate to the smallest possible bulk. Hence, conclusions only are given—reasons and authorities are rarely alluded to.

Justice to myself compels me to add that, while the urgent pressure of professional duties has obliged me to write during brief and scanty intervals only—nevertheless, the ideas advanced are the result of matured convictions, strengthened by several thousand personal examinations of applicants for life insurance.

CHICAGO, 1867. J. A. A.

THE APPLICATION.

The Medical Examiner should first read carefully, point by point, the interrogatories proposed by the Company for which he is acting, and the answers of the applicant. This will save time, and indicate those circumstances which require especial investigation. The form generally adopted, proposes twenty-five questions — twenty-three of which demand the scrutiny of the Examiner. For the purpose of brevity, we adopt the order of the form.

I.

Name, Residence and Occupation.— The name identifies. The residence will suggest at once the nature of the causes of the diseases prevalent, and the relative salubrity of the locality. The moist atmosphere and variable temperature prolific of phthisis; ochlesis, the products of animal decomposition, and foul air, fertile in typhoid fevers and cachexiæ; malarious districts involving endemic diseases which may especially prove noxious to the party, etc., etc.

The Occupation— healthful or pernicious? Statistics show the relative longevity of the different occupations of men, but the Examiner should superadd to these the inquiry: What is the probable effect upon the applicant himself?—for that which is salutiferous to one, is often prejudicial to another. Statistics establish certain general propositions, to which, it must be recollected, many exceptions can be taken.

PROFESSIONAL MEN.—Teachers exhibit the greatest longevity. Next come Clergymen, who are subject to few diseases save those incident to sedentary habits. Contrary to the vulgar opinion, they are not more liable than others to pulmonary affections. Dyspepsia, with its incidents, is their principal affection. Lawyers rank next. Then professional Lecturers, and next, Physicians. Of the latter, it may be said, as a class, they have not the ordinary expectation of life, by from one-third to one-fifth subtraction. Nevertheless, the variety of exposure and habits is such that each case requires isolated investigation.

ARTISTS.—Painters and Sculptors rank among the best risks, particularly when the former sketch from nature, and the latter merely model. Portrait painters, and sculptors who cut marble themselves, are not as good risks. Photographers and Daguerreotypists rank second class.

ARTISANS AND MECHANICS.—Painters using lead and oil are undesirable risks, yet need not be wholly rejected. Workers in phosphorus and quicksilver stand upon the same level. Stone cutters and millers, and similar occupations, where insoluble or irritant particles find constant access to the pulmonary surface, are less desirable, but improved methods of ventilation, now in vogue, render them less objectionable than formerly. Glass blowers are poor risks. Compositors in printing offices signally demand caution in acceptance. Blacksmiths, Furnacemen, Carpenters, Coopers, and Cabinet Makers range among the most healthy operatives. Shoemakers and Harness Makers, mainly from their sedentary habits, are second class risks. The same remark may be made of Tailors. Butchers and Market men, aside from the chances of accident, (to the former particularly,) are good risks. Machinists, Plumbers, Tinsmiths, Tallow Chandlers and Barbers, and similar occupations, are generally good risks. Engravers, Jewelers, and the like, are liable to the diseases of sedentary life, but are otherwise unobjectionable. Brewers, Confectioners, Dyers, Hatters, Bakers, and others whose business involves constant exposure to warm vapors, often impregnated with medicinal or poisonous substances, are not as desirable. Chemists, Assayers, Gilders, Tobacconists, etc., are liable to the same objection. Day Laborers, unless exposed to accident, are equally as good risks as mechanics. Agricultural Laborers, in salubrious localities, are the highest order of desirable applicants.

The best lives, other things being equal, are those of persons engaged in out-door and yet protected employments, where the occupation is somewhat sedentary, and yet combined with a certain amount of muscular exercise, with pure air, and variation enough to secure a stimulating impression upon the system. Inertia, indolence, and absolute uniformity of meteorological influences, are as prejudicial as overexertion and atmospheric vicissitudes.

II.

The Age.— Different ages predispose to particulai diseases. So, also, hereditary diseases, according to their kind, may be outgrown, or not yet arrived at.

During the period of increase, extending to about the twenty-fifth year, (varying, of course, in individuals,) the tendency to disease and death is proportionately very great. One-tenth of all children born die the first month. In large towns, nearly one-half die before the fifth year. Respiratory and strumous diseases are especially fatal between puberty and the age of maturity — placed at twenty-five. None should be insured before puberty, except at extra rates. Between that period and maturity, the party demands especial investigation of the respiratory and glandular systems. Continued fevers, of the typnoid type, are also liable to be destructive during this period. The exanthems readily implant the germs of phthisis and other strumous disorders.

Rheumatism, if it now occurs, in consequence, perhaps, of the excessive activity of the sanguineous system, is exceedingly liable to beget organic disease of the cardiac valves, with its subsequent results.

From the twenty-fifth year to the thirty-fifth, or fortieth, or age of maturity, the best risks, *cæteris paribus*, are chosen. During this period, the applicant stands more, so to speak, on his own individuality. Hereditary predispositions affect him less, and external agencies are easiest resisted when tending to disease The habits and external influences now require mor. careful survey.

From the fortieth year, at latest, decline commences. Hereditary diseases regain their dangerous tendency, and acute affections are met with less power of resistance. Yet, acute diseases of various forms are less to be dreaded than during the mobile years previous to maturity. The progress of changes in the system is slower, and the tendency is to congestions rather than inflammations; to urinary diseases; to fatty degenerations; to cardiac and other obstructions from undue deposits; to dropsies, apoplexies, paralyses, and the like.

The following table shows the expectations, or average duration of life of each individual, calculated from the Carlisle table of mortality:

AGE.	EXPECTATION.	AGE.	EXPECTATION.	AGE.	EXPECTATION.	AGE.	EXPECTATION.
0	38.72	18	42.87	35	31.00	52	19.68
1	44.68	19	42.17	36	30.32	53	18.97
2	47.55	20	41.46	37	29.64	54	18.28
3	49.82	21	40.75	38	28.96	55	17.58
4	50.76	22	40.04	39	28.28	56	16.89
5	51.25	23	39.31	40	27.61	57	16.21
6	51.17	24	38.59	41	26.97	58	15.55
7	50.80	25	37.86	42	26.34	59	14.92
8	50.24	26	37.14	43	25.71	60	14.34
9	49.57	27	36.41	44	25.09	61	13.82
10	48.82	28	35.69	45	24.46	62	13.31
11	48.04	29	35.00	46	23.82	63	12.81
12	47.27	30	34.34	47	23.17	64	12.30
13	46.51	31	33.68	48	22.50	65	11.79
14	45.75	32	33.03	49	21.81	66	11.27
15	45.00	33	32.36	50	21.11	67	10.75
16	44.27	34	31.68	51	20.39	68	10.23
17	43.57						

Other tables vary this expectation from one to two per cent.

But it should be recollected that, in individual cases, the expectation of life may be increased by passing beyond certain ages—a fact wholly ignored by the tables. Thus, for example, where there is clearly an hereditary tendency to phthisis—when parents, or brothers or sisters have died of the disease before twenty-five or thirty, and the party has lived, and is now in good health, at the age of forty, half the danger may be said to have passed; at fifty, three-fourths or four-fifths; and at sixty, but a mere modicum remains—certainly not over one-fifteenth or twentieth, if, indeed, it may be said to exist beyond that of other persons without hereditary predisposition of any sort.

On the contrary, the tendency to gout, urinary diseases, insanity, apoplexy, paralysis, etc., increases with the progress of declining years.

It is safe to say that, when tables indicate a progressive diminution of the life expectation, this idea should be modified and corrected by a full understanding of the hereditary, constitutional, or acquired tendency to, or relief from, special forms of disease.

III.

The Marriage Relation suggests hygienic influences so obvious that it is unnecessary to delay in its con sideration. Married men are usually the most desirable risks. General statistics show that even with females, the dangers incident to maternity do not materially impair the risk. A woman who has once borne a child with no extraordinary difficulty, is a better risk than the *primipara*, and married women than those who are unfortunately single. The circumstances of previous labors, if any have occurred, should be fully understood, and reference had, if possible, to the attending physician.

In large towns and cities, applications are frequently made by those *neither married nor single*, for insurance. These applications are not infrequently made by "housekeepers," who, having passed the heyday of their years without physical impairment, save that which years may bring, become solicitous of providing by endowment for later old age, or else for the support of dependants. These cases are not desirable, neither is it necessary utterly to refuse them. But the most rigid investigation is requisite before they are recommended.

IV. & V.

Sobriety and Temperance — Use of Opium, etc. —

The habitual drinker of alcoholic spirits, or the habitual opium-eater, should, as a rule, be rejected. The inquiry proposed to the applicant will rarely secure a correct answer. Very few will voluntarily admit either intemperance, gluttony, or other generally recognized vice. The Medical Examiner is expected to guard the interests of the Company and co-insurers, by observing carefully the signs of excessive stimulation, as, unfortunately, too often furnished by votaries of Alcohol, Opium, Chloroform, Ether, Cannabis Indica, and the like. The consumption of other stimulants and narcotics besides alcohol, has notably — we might well say *enormously*—increased within several years past. The alcoholic breath is readily detected, but equally clear to the educated perception is the effect of other narcotics and stimulants. Too often the applicant is induced to apply for assurance, by self-consciousness of his indulgence in some pernicious method of excitement, which he knows tends to shorten life, but which he vaguely believes he can abandon or control before it is too late.

INTEMPERANCE, by which we mean not merely drunkenness, but an inordinate, pernicious habit of stimulation by *something*, is, as likely as rheumatism, gout, insanity, or tuberculosis, to be *hereditary*.

The family history here becomes noteworthy. A tuberculous tendency may be, to a certain extent, controlled by hygienic influences; among which may be numbered the use of stimulants of various kinds. The rule for the Medical Examiner is this: If the stimulant taken invigorates digestion and assimilation, then it is not cause for rejection: if it merely excites the nervous system, it is an objection to the risk. *Observe* — invigoration of digestion and assimilation (real power) is not to be confounded with mere increase of adipose tissue, which is often indicative of depression of nutritive energy.

Is the party an occasional or an habitual tippler? There are some men who indulge in only an infrequent debauch, and in the interim are strictly temperate. Such a habit, if ascertained, impairs materially the risk.

The habitual drunkard is well described by Dr. Brinton: "The chief characteristics one can briefly express in words, are the fiery, unctuous skin, with its secretions reeking with volatile, fatty acids; the red and ferrety eyes, with their fitful glare, rather than gleam; the furred tongue; the fetid breath, and the trembling limbs, that often announce the impression made by the copious habitual ingestion of alcohol on the stomach and nervous system respectively."

Other suggestive appearances are afforded by sunken eyes surrounded by dark circles; pallid, or even waxy complexion; moist, *sticky* skin; emaciation; tremulousness of the muscles, unless rendered temporarily tense by a full dose of the stimulant; a nervous restlessness of the whole person; often abstraction of mind, etc., etc. Many times the party will temporarily conceal the habit, or even persuade himself it does not exist to an injurious extent; hence the necessity for great caution. The friend's certificate here becomes indispensable, and the attending physician's testimony should not be overlooked.

Habitual opium-eating does not show such easily described and unmistakable marks, yet can rarely be concealed from an observer of ordinary sagacity, whose attention is directed to the point.

Notwithstanding the singular character of the testimony in the Earl of Mar's case, in England, in 1832, it is safe to say that opium-eating lessens the expectation of life, and is, therefore, a valid reason for declining the risk. Undue nervous irritability; a peculiar, shuffling gait; flabby muscles; drooping eyebrows, with dark lower lids, while the eye itself seems to sink and grow dim; with general marks of old age; or else, while the stimulant has full effect, excitement with brilliant eyes, but contracted pupils; quick, restless movements; or, sometimes, in different temperaments, general dullness, lassitude, sleepiness, and a relaxed skin, with *sticky* perspiration, and husky voice. When the applicant says he has a diarrhœa or dysenteric difficulty which requires *occasional* doses of opium, when the eyes are hazy, and the tongue has a whitish coat; when there is a mucous secretion from the eyes, with frequent hawking of mucus from a flabby mucous membrane of the pharynx, and perhaps of the nose. When he is a married man, and with these symptoms, has no children, carefully observe and reject him. Much must be left to professional discretion — but *cave canem*.

VI.

Vaccinated? — A person who has never been vaccinated or had the small pox, should not be accepted. If vaccinated, the inquiry should be: Was the vaccination successful? and then, how recently was the operation performed? A successful vaccination many years previous, is not sufficient, but if it has been frequently repeated without infection, the case may be deemed clear. In doubtful cases, examine the cicatrix, or re-vaccinate at once. If small pox or varioloid has occurred, it requires especial caution as to the condition of the lungs and intestinal mucous membrane. The date when it occurred should be given, and the fact of perfect or imperfect recovery noted.

VII. & VIII.

Residence in a Foreign Climate.— Without exact reference to isothermal lines, natives of the zone extending from the thirtieth to the fiftieth parallels of latitude, may be considered as the best risks. An acquaintance with the meteorological condition of particular localities, is of great importance. Excessive thermometrical, barometrical and hygrometrical variations, in any particular locality, usually impair risks, by rendering them subject to various diseases.

Thus, moist, warm situations usually involve the malarious diseases; cold, or variable, and moist regions are prolific of tuberculous cachexiæ; dry (yet variable in temperature) districts, render rheumatic and inflammatory diseases more dangerous. On equal parallels, the temperature of Europe is higher than that of America, and excepting the influence of the changes produced by cultivation, present the diseases of lower climates in higher latitudes. General temperaments are varied by persistent climatic influences. (*Vid.* p. 61, *et seq.*)

ACCLIMATION IN THE SOUTH.--—Whilst men, almost alone of animals, can range from the Equator to the "open Polar Sea," with apparent impunity, by observing certain precautions which their reason and knowledge suggest, nevertheless, they subject themselves, sooner or slower, to organic changes which are termed briefly "acclimation." These changes render them less iable to the acute diseases of localities, or endemics but they are fraught with much significance to the insurance examiner.

More than two thousand years ago, the naturalist Pliny noticed that "those who are seasoned can live amid pestilential diseases." The reason of this may be a matter of speculation, but of its essential truth there can be no doubt. The organic changes thus brought about express themselves in the larger phase of different races of men, begotten through the operation of ages of similar influences acting on parent and progeny.

Without descending to minutiæ, it may be said the Northerner going South may become, to a certain extent, acclimated by physical changes in the skin, liver and spleen, especially involving their heightened activity of interstitial change, and, usually, increase in bulk. Increased activity of any organ, according to a well known natural law, involves greater tendency to disease. If, instead of more energetic action of the skin, there is less, from any temporary or permanent cause, then the mucous membrane of the intestine will be called into excessive activity, and the acute or chronic diarrhœa of tropical climates be produced. Else there are the "bloated belly, distorted features, dark yellow complexion, livid eyes and lips; in short, all the symptoms of dropsy, jaundice and ague, united in one person."

Coming North, the comparatively healthy Southron falls an easy victim to tuberculous, nephritic, and inflammatory diseases. The rule is to observe the relative activity and development of each organ or apparatus involved — whatever the cause of variation.

Acclimation to the so-called malarious fevers, etc., of the South, gives no immunity to YELLOW FEVER, any more than does typhoid fever from variola at the North. Yellow fever is a disease of cities and towns epidemic usually, and requires its especial prophylaxis — not gained by any mere acclimation. As Dr. Nott emphatically writes: "The citizen of the town is fully acclimated to *its* atmosphere, but cannot spend a single night in the country without serious risk of life; nor can the squalid, liver-stricken countryman come into the city during the prevalence of yellow fever, without danger of dying with black vomit."

The immunity from second attacks of yellow fever is nearly complete, yet the constitution is liable to permanent impairment from its ravages, and in all cases organic diseases are carefully to be looked for.

The immunity from diseases prevalent in particular localities often exhibited, in exceptional cases, is due principally to two causes: *First*, The peculiar organization of the individual himself; and, *Second*, The care with which he adapts his life, manners and customs to his changed surroundings. As Dr. Hammond remarks: "For an Englishman or an American to attempt a residence in latitude 80° without changing his food, clothing or habits, by making them conform to the climate to which he has come, would lead to but one termination — death. But if he studies the conditions by which he is surrounded, and profits by the experience of those to whom it is natural, he becomes habituated to the new order of things, and lives in health and comfort."

The same law holds good with reference to a change to hot climates. Hence, he who has shown, by actual experience, that he has maintained good health in either extreme of latitude, may be more safely insured, or, if already insured, be granted permission, more readily, to take up a Northern or Southern residence.

Nearly the same law holds good with regard to yellow fever or other epidemic disease — the best prophylaxis is for the individual so to shape his habits as *to keep well* — and he who will attempt this, is the best risk.

IX. & X.

Employed in the Army or Navy? — The careful examination to which the recruit is ordinarily subjected before being mustered into the service, is a point in his favor, if he was received. Questions then arise as to the influence of the service upon him. The diseases to which he has generally been exposed are principally "typho-malarial fever," rubeola, camp diarrhœa, dysentery, rheumatism, scorbutus, pneumonia, catarrh, cardiac changes, Bright's disease, and not least, venereal affections.

An individual who has escaped permanent systemic or organic disorder, from these various causes, may generally be put down as a good risk, even though his personal or family history is not every way satisfactory. Nevertheless, the *obscure results*, often capable of discovery on rigid examination, require more than usual care, before accepting the applicant.

In my own experience, I have often found cardiac and renal diseases, and the secondary or tertiary forms of syphilis in returned soldiers, discoverable only after most careful scrutiny. The exposures and exigencies of the service involve the most potent causes of organic disease, even though the elasticity of many systems prevents immediate manifestation of striking symptoms.

PREVIOUS EMPLOYMENTS, AND THEIR EFFECT ON HEALTH.—The present occupation may be ordinarily innoxious, but the previous employments have left lasting traces of injurious influence. So, again, the present business may be such as to endanger the health generated by previous healthful engagements. The peculiarities of the individual here require cautious investigation. (*Vid. Occupation.*)

XI.
Has the Party had any of the following Diseases?

Apoplexy,
Asthma,
Bronchitis,
Consumption,
Cholic,
Diphtheria,
Disease of the Heart,
Dropsy,
Fits,
Fistula,
Gout,
Insanity,
Liver Complaint,
Paralysis,
Palpitation,
Quinsy,
Rheumatism
Rupture,
Scarlet Fever,
Spitting of Blood,
Diseases of the Urinary Organs.

Seriatim.—A party who has had a decided attack of APOPLEXY should be rejected. Evident tendency thereto also should disqualify.

ASTHMA is but a symptom—it may or may not be a cause of absolute rejection. Each case requires specific examination.

Observe—Asthma may occur merely from local irritants applied to the respiratory surface, and the causes of such local irritation may depend upon mere idiosyncrasy. Or it may depend upon blood poisoning of various kinds. Thus particles of hay, soot, excessive moisture, atoms of certain gases, anima. emanations, ipecacuanha and other medicinal substances are capable of producing more or less severe spasmodic asthma. Such cases, irrespective of organic lesion, do not necessarily disqualify from insurance. Some persons always have asthma in certain localities—never in others. Thus C. cannot stay a single night in Ann Arbor, Mich., without a severe paroxysm of asthma; yet he has lived years in Detroit, only 37 miles distant, without a single attack. A., well known to me, lives in California with perfect health and freedom from the disease, whereas, in the Northern United States, he is a constant sufferer. These individual peculiarities, and the suffering they generate, are the best guarantee that the party will himself protect the interests of the Company. Nearly the same remark may be made with reference to asthma from blood poisoning—prominent among the causes of which we may mention malaria, or such other causes as promote portal venous congestion. Alcoholic stimulants, and sometimes even unexpected articles, as sugar, will occasionally produce the same result. Here the persistence of the cause must govern the judgment. None of these cases wholly preclude acceptance of the risk.

Again, asthma may depend upon reflex causes totally independent of permanent organic disease. It may alternate with ague, or other periodical disorders It may depend on uterine, vesical, rectal, or even gastric disorder. It may be dependent solely on an excitable temperament and emotional influences. The gravity and permanence of the excito-motor cause here must be sought out, and only its due importance attached. But Asthma, which is the symptom of *cardiac obstruction* — of *tuberculosis* — of *emphysema* — of acute or chronic *bronchitis* — of *thoracic tumors* — or, perhaps, *aneurism* — of *hepatic venous obstruction* from thoracic disease, or parenchymatous change in the liver itself — or from *organic cerebral* or *spinal change*, should utterly preclude insurance.

BRONCHITIS.—A proclivity to attacks of bronchitis should disqualify, not only from the dangers of uncomplicated bronchitis, but because it is so often symptomatic of the tuberculous diathesis. Again, as indicative of nephritic, cardiac, gastric, or other diseases of remote organs, or those from septic causes, (typhoid, syphilis, etc.) It may be observed, however, that bronchitis may, and often does, leave a condensation of a portion of the pulmonary vesicular structure, simulating tubercular deposit, and again, that it may leave behind dilatations of the tubes, which simulate very closely excavations from tubercular softening. Resulting emphysema should be carefully searched for, and its fallacious resonance not confounded with healthy lung-vesicular structure. Popularly, simple pharyngitis, and all slight or severe catarrhal inflammations, are merged in the general term bronchitis; so that the information conveyed by the patient's own statement is of very little practical value.

CONSUMPTION.—The rule is absolute that consumptive cases should be rejected. Physical investigation is always to be exact, for the healthiest external appearance may but hide the germs of the disease.

CHOLIC.—This term indicates but a symptom, the significance of which depends solely upon its cause. Taken in its widest sense, we may say that at the present time, improved methods of diagnosis and treatment, have robbed the disease of its formerly dangerous character, and unless proceeding from peculiar causes, it need not be considered a cause for rejection. The well known forms are the gastric, intestinal, hepatic, nephritic, and that from lead, or, perhaps, also, copper poisoning. The cholic of flatulency, or temporary dyspepsia, does not particularly enhance the risk — neither does the so-called bilious cholic, unless the patient is peculiarly subject to it. If, however, the latter evidently depends upon the passage of gall-stones, and frequently recurs, it is a cause for rejection. Where painter's, or other metallic cholic has occurred, it is not, alone, to be considered cause for rejection, unless it has *recurred*, and particularly, the same occupation has been continued. The lead worker who has had this cholic, and continues in the business, should be rejected. A single attack of nephritic cholic need not reject — recurrence, even at a distant interval of time, should exclude. Many so called cases of cholic are really enteritis, and may indicate *marasmus*. The local and general evidences of tuberculosis of the mesenteric glands, must be investigated.

CARDIAC DISEASE.—Organic disease of the heart positively excludes. Physical diagnosis is indispensable here, but it should be recollected that, as a rule, while the healthy heart may, from accidental causes, give an abnormal sound temporarily, the heart diseased to such an extent as to reject, can not, for any continuous period, give forth healthy sounds. Abnormality in rhythm or impulse may depend solely upon temporary causes, and so, also, may abnormality of sound — but when these are present, the parts should always be re-examined. Variations in rhythm or impulse may be individual peculiarities, and there are evidences that varied sounds may also depend upon idiosyncrasy, but the safer rule is never to accept the party, unless the natural sounds may be heard. When, from any cause, cardiac disease has *frequently* occurred, and abnormalities are present, the party should be turned over to invalid companies.

DROPSY.—This is another symptom which may, or may not, be of importance. If present at the time of examination, no chances should be taken, but the party advised to postpone the application. It may have been a sequence of malarious disease — as often from ague — if there be not now malarial cachexia, it is no cause of rejection — but if hepatic or splenic parenchymatous disease remain, the applicant should be rejected or postponed until that is cured. It may have been left behind by scarlatina, or other zymotic disease — if it has not recurred, and the evidence of nephritic, cardiac, or other organic disease do not remain, it is not cause for rejection. It may have resulted from peritonitis, which has been entirely recovered from — if so, the party may be received. If from *chronic* peritonitis, it is cause for rejection. If it occurs from *renal* (Bright's) disease, from permanent *hepatic*, *cardiac*, or *pulmonary* organic affection, the party cannot be assured. The dropsy from drunkard's liver, (*cirrhosis*) vitiates the application.

Aside from constitutional causes, the effusion into the pericardium is more grave in insurance prognosis, than that into the pleural cavity. The latter than ascites, and ascites than that into the areolar tissue, œdema, anasarca, etc. But local anasarca always necessitates the greatest care, lest *albuminuria* be present or impending, or lest some permanent organic disease is its origin. Any constitutional cachexia, as syphilis, in connection with the dropsical effusion, even though organic disease may not be discovered, precludes insurance.

DIPHTHERIA, aside from its immediate danger, may lay the foundation of *tuberculosis* — may be followed by *albuminuria* or dropsical effusions, or more or less permanent *paralysis*. It is not usually mentioned in the list of diseases about which the party is questioned, but its grave sequelæ entitle it to thorough consideration.

FISTULA. — Fistulæ are of importance, as indicative of local or general disease, or both. Locally, they may indicate the presence of a foreign substance at the bottom, as more particularly a bit of dead bone, or cartilage. In each of these instances the surgical pathology becomes the prime point of inquiry.

The cause and extent of the necrosis whether of bone or cartilage. The location of the bullet, or splinter, bit of cloth, or whatever it may be. The surgical curability of the salivary, fæcal, urinary, etc., false outlet, with the question of its cause. So also of the mechanical action of muscles. The importance of the organ reached by the fistulous opening may have much to do with the decision of the case, *e. g.* bone, gland. Some Life Companies vaguely instruct their examiners that Fistulæ are a positive cause of rejection. In this case FISTULA IN ANO is, evidently, the difficulty intended. But whether *fistula in ano* should reject depends wholly upon its cause and extent.

First — If it is among the signs of tuberculosis, it should certainly reject — whatever opinion may be entertained as to its hastening or retarding the tuberculous development.

Second — If it has proved obstinate under correct treatment, it should disqualify.

Third — If it is large, burrowing, and exhausting, it is ample cause for rejection.

But if it is traceable to ulceration of the part from merely local or temporary causes, as hæmorrhoids, acute dysentery, or direct mechanical injury — *without* evidences of the tuberculous diathesis, or remote organic disease — if it has proved amenable to appropriate treatment, and is no longer a cause of exhaustion, it should not reject the risk. Personally, the opinion of the writer is that, with the improved surgical methods of the present time, too much significance has been attached to this *usually* strictly local difficulty.

FITS.—Under this general and vague designation, the insurance forms prominently intend *Epilepsy* in its various phases. When Epilepsy is clearly present, whatever its degree or frequency of manifestation, it utterly disqualifies. Not that it necessarily shortens life *per se*, but because even without this usual result it may impair the mental faculties, or dispose to accidents, which essentially impair the risk. The epileptiform convulsions of primary dentition, and the changes incident to that epoch, if they have not manifested a disposition to return, or injured the mental faculties, or involved paralyses, in later life do not disqualify. The irregular muscular contractions of simple Hysteria, unless connected with organic disease, or general cachexia, do not prevent acceptance. Males of nervous temperament sometimes manifest symptoms very like those of Hysteria with its queer symptoms—such cases should be carefully investigated, but these symptoms do not necessarily disqualify. Youths of both sexes about and after the age of puberty for several years may exhibit mild or severe epileptiform symptoms, or even decided periodical convulsions, yet if these either spontaneously, or under treatment subside, it may be laid down as a rule that if after several years they do not recur, the risk is a good one. The age of twenty-five in the male and twenty-three in the female may be considered *critical* in this regard.

CHOREA, in all particulars, may be regarded as identical with the "*fits*," of the formulary, so far as its pathology and influence upon longevity is concerned.

GOUT, of chronic character, and particularly, if in any degree hereditary, disqualifies. But it does not follow that all sore toes are gouty. Analysis of individual cases is indispensable. The habits of life, and surroundings, will attract the attention of the examiner. The Dyspepsia and general *malaise* discoverable by examination are of more significance to the cautious medical agent of the Company.

INSANITY does not always tend to shorten life directly, but if present disqualifies on account, *first*, of disease of central nervous organs which it indicates: and, *second*, because of the greater liability to accidental death which the withdrawal of healthful reason involves. It is to be distinguished from the delirium of temporary disease, and from mere eccentricity. Malarious diseases are not infrequently followed by an interval of insanity, sometimes of the most active character, and yet which recovered from tends not an hour to shorten life. Of this the writer's personal experience has given him abundant evidences. Such cases need not necessarily be rejected. The puerperal state often, also, involves this condition with similar prognosis; but if puerperal insanity have occurred, it is better not to insure unless the grand climacteric has been passed. Hereditary insanity, and a single attack in the individual, or marked proclivity thereto, or where it is as evident in the family connection as other hereditary diseases adverted to should reject. The well balanced mind cannot contemplate suicide without horror, but the evidences are abundant that oftentimes murder and suicide may be the only manifestations of the hereditary taint of insanity, and, therefore, although pregnant signs of mania in any of its forms may be absent, and general good health apparent, the risk should nevertheless, in such cases, be declined. Yet justice to applicants requires, when insanity is mentioned as having occurred in the connection, that the particulars of the case be inquired into. It may occur that the instance was one from some incidental, and not hereditary cause. It may have arisen from local injury, from septic poisoning of the blood, or, perhaps, have been merely senile mental decay, etc., in either instance, not invalidating the risk. Other things being equal, the actual presence of insanity will lessen the chances of longevity to one-fifth or one-sixth the healthy standard.

LIVER COMPLAINT.—Hepatic diseases are to be looked for in those who are, or have been residents of malarious districts; in spirit drinkers; and those of the technical bilious temperament. 1. *Enlargement of the liver*, if from *portal venous congestion*, may not invalidate the risk; if from *hepatic venous congestion*, it is a sign of disease pregnant with danger, and while present should absolutely reject. The hobnail or drunkards' liver (cirrhosis) should reject. As an isolated symptom, the contracted or small liver is more suspicious than the enlarged one. Persistent hepatic disorder, points prominently to tuberculosis, fatty degeneration, cirrhosis, or malignant diseases, either of which will disqualify. Adjacent tumors may, more or less, permanently, obstruct the passage of bile, or directly interfere with the action of the organ. Of course, these should reject. Abscesses present reject; but, if formerly existent, and now fully recovered from, are to be judged of from their causes and effect upon the system. The abscess, from local or accidental cause, has less significance than that from pyæmia; the latter than that from abnormal deposit, as of tubercle, cancer, etc. Recurring abscesses disqualify, whatever the cause. A tendency to the formation of *gall-stones*, with ileus or jaundice, if recurrent, should be an obstacle to approval.

JAUNDICE, while present, *postpones* acceptance. If dependent on *hepatic venous congestion*, it rejects. If it depended simply on *portal congestion*, as occuring in malarial or other fevers, it is comparatively trivial. Observe, it is only a *symptom*, and its real meaning necessitates examination and judgment. Thus it may appear as a consequence of a catarrhal condition of the bile ducts; or as the result of impaction of gall-stone, or the mechanical pressure of tumors; fæcal accumulations in the colon; from lumbricoid worms in the common duct, etc. Or it may be an evidence of malignant degeneration, or of permanent organic disease, as tuberculous, fibroid, fatty or amyloid degeneration, etc. From the largely more frequent causes of this symptom being temporary, and not permanent in operation, the isolated symptom may be considered as suggestive of investigation, and not as a reason by itself for rejection.

PARALYSIS, whether simply local, paraplegic, or hemiplegic, demands the most scrupulous examination. Hemiplegia or paraplegia, if present, totally disqualify. But if formerly present, as clearly the result of some merely temporarily acting cause, and this cause has been entirely removed, *e. g.* infantile neurosis, accidental lesion, hysteria, etc., it may be passed over. When combined with cardiac disease, or the apoplectic diathesis, even though there be apparent health, it should reject. The import of the local cause is the important point of inquiry. Local paralysis may occur from local injury, local tumor, or similar cause, and not disqualify. When present, and not clearly explicable as the result of a removable or innoxious local cause, it should reject.

PALPITATION of the heart is a symptom of little significance. Always noted among the list of symptoms about which the patient is questioned, it really is of no importance, save as directing attention toward organic disease of the heart, or toward dyspepsia or disorders of innervation. Taken by itself, it is a symptom which attracts attention to its possible cause, but neither accepts nor rejects.

QUINSY, or Tonsillitis. This local affection is principally important as one of the evidences of the tuberculous diathesis. It is capable, it is true, of producing death by mechanical occlusion of the respiratory passages, but this is so rare an accident that, practically, it may be neglected in calculating the chances of the risk. The same remark may be made as with reference to the danger of lancing the swollen tonsils. By this little operation, branches of the carotid artery may be wounded, and death result, just as death may result from choking while eating. But when the party admits being subject to this difficulty, local examination should be made with the tongue spatula, or better still, the laryngoscope.

RHEUMATISM. — Frequent and aggravated attacks of rheumatism, even though important internal organs may not have been previously involved, should disqualify. Hereditary rheumatism impairs the risk. It is a disease, so far as danger is concerned, characterized by its tendency to affect particularly the white fibrous tissues. Thus, the cardiac valves, the pericardium, the dura mater, etc., become liable to fatal change. Uric and sulphuric acids are largely abundant in the secretions, and the blood becomes abnormally fibrinous. The real danger of this diathesis is, in the first place, from acute changes which may involve speedy dissolution, or from deposits which necessitate grave organic disease which may, later, cause sudden or gradual death. It is capable also of so exhausting the blood itself, as to render the risk a bad one, irrespective of organic change.

In judging of the effects of the organic diathesis, the atmospheric vicissitudes, and the habits of life of the party must be noted; next, the ordinary condition of the skin and kidneys; then, *most assiduously*, the irritability, or actual organic cnange of the heart structures; then, the continuance and frequency of return of the symptoms.

Most patients when questioned with regard to the presence of rheumatism, will refer to occasional pains in the muscles, or stiffness in the joints, of a *quasi* rheumatic character, as being true rheumatism; the Examiner must observe that these are not intended by the question, else, no person could be considered as exempt. Acute rheumatism, or a decidedly rheumatic diathesis, is what is to be looked after. A single attack of even inflammatory rheumatism may not disqualify, although it may have been severe. But if *metastatic*, it should militate against the risk. If recurrent, as well as metastatic, it should reject. If the case has been *progressive*, and without being *metastatic*, has passed on from point to point, and ultimately involved the heart, the insurance prognosis is more grave than in case of mere temporary metastasis. Mere thickening of fasciæ or stiffening of the joints from long previous, but not recurrent rheumatism, need not impair the risk—neither lumbago, nor even, so-called, sciatica of a clearly chronic rheumatic origin; but when local paralyses, or temporary or permanent symptoms of apoplexy have resulted, the risk should be rejected. Coagula may be condensed on the roughened cardiac surfaces, and their detachment from time to time determine local paralysis, apoplexiæ or even mortification, to the extreme astonishment of the superficially informed.

Chronic Catarrhal Affections—sometimes paroxysmal in character, are often of rheumatic or gouty origin, so also, sclerotitis and even meningitis and maniacal delirium. The *quasi* rheumatism of malarious districts requires particular examination, and so also, those varieties resulting from gonorrhœa and syphilis—each of which may puzzle the practitioner, but must be isolated to judge of its influence upon longevity.

Metastatic rheumatism rejects; syphilitic rheumatism rejects; especially does recurrent rheumatism of hereditary character reject; chronic sciatica of intense character rejects—so also, does severe lumbago, tic doloureux, etc. Whenever rheumatism is acute or chronic, long continued, recurrent, hereditary or accompanied with cachexia, the insurance company must have the benefit of the doubt which naturally arises, and the party be declined.

Rheumatism is liable to be confounded in diagnosis with erysipelas, gout, trichinous disease and neuralgia; especially is it liable to be mistaken for phthisis, pleurisy, etc., when occurring in the intercostal muscles. Scorbutic pains are very liable to be mistaken for chronic rheumatism. In prognosis, not more than one or two per cent. prove fatal, directly or remotely, and half of these of the latter result. At the present time, from improved methods of treatment, it may be confidently asserted that the disease has been robbed of half of its individual terror, and in its insurance, direct or remote, prognosis, of three-quarters of its significance.

RUPTURE.—The frequency of Hernia in its different forms, and its inherently dangerous nature, renders this point one never to be overlooked. According to the most general statistics, hernia is to be found in an average of one to every fifteen of the adult population. It is about fourteen times more frequent in males than females, although in the latter it is more dangerous, as they are more subject to the crural form, and again, because from motives of delicacy, they do not as early apply for relief. Hernia progressively diminishes in frequency from birth till puberty, and then progressingly increases with advancing age. Viz: First year — 1 in 21; second year — 1 in 29; third year — 1 in 37; until at the thirteenth year it falls to 1 in 77. Shortly after this, its frequency rises again; thus, at the twenty-first year there is 1 case in 32; at the twenty-eighth year — 1 in 21; at the thirty-fifth year — 1 in 17; at the fortieth year — 1 in 9; at the fiftieth year — 1 in 6; from sixty to seventy years 1 in 4; from seventy to seventy-five years — 1 in 3. In women it occurs most frequently during the child bearing years. Umbilical and direct hernia are less dangerous than the inguinal or crural forms; the latter more so than the inguinal. The irreducible is more objectionable than the reducible; and *always*, where a truss, of suitable construction fails to prevent descent of the intestine, the risk should be rejected. Cases of *double* hernia should always be rejected. *Observe* — Occasionally parties suppose they have hernia, when there is simply an enlarged gland, or a fatty tumor, retained testis, hydrocele, etc. Accuracy of diagnosis is here indispensable to protect the rights both of the company and the applicant. Hernia, whether single or double, which has been operated upon and apparently cured, it should be remembered, is liable to recur on gradual absorption of the new formation. This fact will have weight in properly classifying the risk.

SCARLET FEVER.— The larger proportion of cases of scarlatina occur before the insurable age. When it occurs in the adult, its secondary results demand most cautious examination. These not rarely involve breaking down of the constitution, or serious local organic changes, which imperil the risk, and this, although the primary attack may have been apparently mild. Taking all the cases together, the mortality from scarlatina is scarcely exceeded by that of any other single form of disease. Consumption and typhoid fever, (including typhus,) only outrank it in fatality. It is said to be even more fatal in Europe than in this country. Fatal as it is in the onset, the medical examiner has more to do with its subsequent ravages upon the system; and these, it is found, principally depend on primary obstructions to the functional action of the kidneys. Hence, uræmia, albuminuria, anasarca, dropsy, etc. Again, its local affection of the eustachian tube, and ear may ultimate in destructive caries of the bones, and eventually prove fatal by lesion of the brain. Thus a chronic ottorrhœa, originating from this cause, militates against the risk, although it may not alone positively reject. Of course albuminuria, etc., reject. If the party has had scarlet fever and fully recovered from it, the risk is improved thereby. Many of the Continental Europeans reply to the examiner that they have had scarlet fever, or that some of their family have died of it, when on careful questioning, it will be found that "maculated typhus" is the disease intended.

Again, many cases of slight roseolar eruption are confounded with it. Such cases render it necessary for interrogation to be minute and exact in all doubtful instances.

SPITTING OF BLOOD.— Unexplained *Hæmoptysis* is one of the most pitilessly exclusive of historical symptoms. Primarily, because it is one of the earliest precursors of phthisis, and, again, because it tokens its actual existence. So large is the proportion of those exhibiting this symptom whose lives, sooner or later, terminate by consumption, that it is unnecessary to argue from recorded experience, or to appeal to the abundant statistics which have accumulated. Absence of the tubercular taint in the family history, or of concurrent signs in the individual, will not explain it away. Absence of physical signs is scarcely more to be regarded, under such circumstances, than those of the rational sort. The proof must be *positive* that the spitting of blood came from other cause than incipient or present tuberculosis of the lungs. *Negative evidences are in no case sufficient. It must be proved* that the blood came from the gums, the nares, the pharynx, the œsophagus or stomach. Or it *must be proved* that it came from the accidentally abraded larynx, trachea or bronchi; or that it depended solely on mechanical or surgical injury of the vesicular lung structure; or that it depended solely on *vicarious* causes. Dr. Aitken emphatically observes: "Cases are recorded of its so-called idiopathic occurrence, as from variations (suddenly) of atmospheric pressure, ascending high mountains, or descending in diving bells, violent straining efforts, or from plethora; but in such cases, according to the experience of Drs. Fuller, Walshe and others, 'there is usually some latent mischief in the chest — some local cause of pulmonary congestion — some mechanical interference with the capillary circulation through the lungs.'" Finally—we observe that it may depend upon disease of the heart, especially with mitral regurgitation; upon aneurism; upon intra-thoracic tumors, either malignant or non-malignant; or upon non-tubercular abscesses. But, in either case, it rejects as decidedly as though dependent on tuberculosis.

Hæmatemesis, a symptom often confounded with hæmoptysis, is of vastly less significance, nevertheless requires, from its occasionally dangerous origin, very careful inquiry as to its real cause. The blood may have come from the nares, the throat *or the lungs*, have been swallowed and vomited. It may have come from aneurism above or below the stomach, from malignant or non-malignant gastric ulcer; occasionally as the result of severe gastritis; again as vicarious of menstrual or other discharges. In the vast majority of cases it occurs as the result of the local congestions of malarious diseases, or from scorbutus or purpura. The decomposed blood, or coffee-grounds vomit of yellow fever, etc., need hardly be alluded to.

DISEASES OF THE URINARY ORGANS.— Under this euphemistic designation are intended—nephritis, nephralgia, cystitis, stone in the bladder, diabetes, hæmaturia, albuminuria or Bright's disease, prostatitis, spermatorrhœa, gonorrhœa, stricture, urinary fistula, syphilis, or other organic or constitutional diseases

involving the urinary organs, *primarily* or *secondarily*.
The question is last but not least. The obscurities
of diagnosis and prognosis are more frequently hidden
here than in any other part of the animal frame work,
and coincidently, here, the acuteness of the medical examiner
will be taxed even more than in the minutely
studied and carefully described changes of the thoracic
viscera. For the physical signs are clear to the moderately
educated perceptive faculties, whilst both physical
and rational signs exhaust the skill of diagnosis
when the renal and subsidiary organs come under
view. *Chronic nephritis* rejects, and so also, chronic
nephralgia, whatever their causes. *Cystitis*, if present,
rejects, whether acute or chronic. *Calculus* rejects;
but the previous passage of a small concretion may
not disqualify, unless the diathesis be strongly marked,
and the evidences be strengthened by hereditary predisposition.
Diabetes necessarily rejects, but doubtful
cases should be analyzed. *Albuminuria*, or *Bright's
disease* in any of its forms, absolutely rejects.
Observe — that organic disease of the kidneys may be
present without albuminuria, and albuminuria may
occur without renal organic change, but either, if
present, reject. *Prostatitis*, or the prostatic enlargement
of old age, if sufficient to materially interfere
with the extrusion of urine, must reject. *Spermatorrhœa*,
so-called, is usually merely a catarrh of the
urinary mucous membrane, analogous to the leuchorrhœa
of females, and of trivial importance. It is
usually an evidence either of mere dyspeptic derangement,
or of improper medication. Notwithstanding
the stress laid upon it by many authorities, it is safe

to say that, in at least nineteen cases out of twenty, it in no wise invalidates the risk. True spermatorrhœa will manifest itself in connection with other symptoms involving the constitution as a whole, which will require no reference to this as necessary to sustain an opinion. Taken as a symptom, isolated, it is of as little importance as a nasal catarrh. The previous occurence of *Gonorrhœa* is mainly of importance because its old time treatment, by balsamic and other highly irritant remedies, may have laid the foundation of Bright's disease; or because it may have been followed by septic poisoning of the blood, involving gonorrhœal rheumatism, etc. This latter is capable of producing organic diseases, of equal importance with those of rheumatism from the usually more noted causes. *Stricture*, whether the result of gonorrhœa or accidental causes, requires attention. Is it spasmodic or permanent? Is it permeable or impermeable? Is it the result of merely a local or of a remote cause? It is often times symptomatic of renal or vesical organic disease, and these disqualify. If trivial, although troublesome, it is of less importance. If it require Syme's, or other severe operation for its relief, the insurance should be postponed. A similar remark may be made of urinary fistula. Let it be cured, whatever its cause, before insurance. All malignant diseases of the organs of course reject. *In all cases of renal or urinary disease*, ONCE MORE, *examine the heart.*

SYPHILIS.—In all cases where secondary or tertiary syphilis is clearly present the risk should be postponed. This disease is usually capable of perfect cure. In badly managed or cachectic cases it becomes dangerous to longevity. At the present time it is better managed, and the chances of perfect recovery are better than heretofore. But the rule is imperative—*when present, reject.* Observe, historically, the distinction between the merely local sore, (however extensive its ravages) the chancroid, and the true infecting chancre— the latter only of insurance import. The best disposed party applying for insurance will perhaps deny its previous occurrence, and there may be no signs superficially to be observed. And yet it is easy for the moderately instructed examiner, in the majority of instances, to satisfy himself of the facts. Nevertheless, the present writer admits the loss of one risk for which he was examiner, by giving credit to the party's own statement and innocent countenance. Many cases of reported consumption, for whose demise the examiner is held professionally responsible, are in fact, syphilitic decline and ultimate decay. But the examiner must guard himself against such disastrous result by stern disregard of appearances. This he can do without violating any of the proprieties. Observe whether there are any traces of cutaneous eruption—whether there is or has been alopecia— whether there is emaciation, or other signs of depraved nutrition, onychia, *enlarged post-cervical glands,* iritis, catarrh, white patches or tubercles, or cicatrices about the mucous membrane of the mouth, tongue or throat; whether there are nodes, or have been pains in the bones. If possible, (perhaps under excuse of examining for hernia), examine for the significant induration of the inguinal glands. Indeed when the attention is directed to the matter, it does not require much tact or sagacity to make up one's mind safely. Fortunately doubtful cases are overrated in importance. It is perhaps necessary to call the attention of the examiner to the general *physiognomy* of urino-genital diseases, which is almost too unmistakable for the expert ever to be deceived in—but for the inexperienced it is proper to say that it is both capable of observation and indescribable.

XII.

HAS THE PARTY HAD INFLAMMATORY RHEUMATISM?
The repetition of this question by several companies in their forms, attests the great importance attached to its satisfactory answer. But sufficient has been written upon this point upon p. 29. *et seq.*

XIII. & XIV.

SUBJECT TO DYSPEPSIA, DYSENTERY OR DIARRHŒA?
A perfect state of health of the alimentary canal and its subsidiary organs is, of course, necessary in order that there should be perfect nutrition of all parts of the body. Temporary disturbances may arise from temporarily acting causes and yet not invalidate the risk; but frequently recurring, or persistent disorder, whatever the cause, throws doubt upon it, and then the case must be carefully diagnosed.

Dyspepsia is primarily noteworthy because it is one of the initiatory symptoms of the tubercular diathesis.

Or it may evidence organic malignant or non-malignant disease of the stomach. It may be sympathetic of cerebral or renal, of uterine or spinal affection of more or less serious character. In the larger proportion of instances it indicates merely a catarrhal condition of the gastric mucous membrane, or slight disturbance of the hepatic functions. But whatever its cause, duration or severity, whenever present, it should receive ample consideration.

Dysentery, when present, rejects, and if the party is subject to its recurrence, enquiry must be made as to its cause and origin. Chronic colitis or enterocolitis reject. But many cases of supposed dysentery depend solely on hæmorrhoids, local, curable ulceration, or morbid growths about the rectum. Nevertheless it is safe to say that tenesmus, discharges of blood and pus, especially with occasional febrile heat and emaciation, should reject. The condition of the liver in such cases, should be carefully observed.

Diarrhœa is a term relative to the habits of the individual. It does not refer so much to the frequency as to the character of the discharges. Occasional attacks of acute diarrhœa may occur in the very best risks. Such cases point to an examination into the habits of the party, whether of eating, drinking or exposure to vicissitudes of temperature, moisture or exercise. Ill regulated diet, imperfect mastication, improper quality of food, irregular hours, and intemperance of drink, are among the most frequent causes,— but some form of enteritis, hepatic derangement, or disease of the glandular organs, subsidiary to the digestive apparatus,— Bright's disease,—*ochlesis*, malaria, with other agencies are capable of producing the same result. The votary of opium or alcoholic stimulants is scarcely ever free from this symptom. In returned soldiers, or those addicted to vegetarian theories, it is frequently the result of *scorbutus*. When there is emaciation, a despondent countenance, dark circles around sunken eyes, a sallow, leaden or sodden skin, a sunken abdomen, a red and pointed, or a loose, pale and flabby tongue,— an undue indifference, or an augmented irritability of the nervous system, *look out for diarrhœa and its cause.*

XV.

HABITUAL COUGH? The significance of an habitual cough in life insurance examinations depends wholly on its cause; but if admitted, it requires critical examination. It may depend on local causes in the pharynx, larynx, trachea, bronchia, or pulmonary parenchyma. It may arise from cardiac, hepatic, gastric, intestinal or spinal disease. It may be a mere morbid habit of the nerves and muscles involved in the act. Primarily, it demands physical diagnosis of the condition of the lung tissue, especially at the apices of the lobes,—together with a rational account of the history and diathesis. Taken as a mere symptom, Dr. Hartshorne's statement is as brief and satisfactory as any which can be given, viz:

Cough is dry and hollow, or hacking, when nervous or sympathetic.
Dry and tight in early bronchitis;
Soft, deep and loose, in advanced bronchitis;
Hacking, in incipient phthisis pulmonalis;

Deep and distressing in confirmed consumption;
Short and sharp in pneumonia;
Barking and hoarse in early or spasmodic croup;
Whistling in advanced membranous croup;
Paroxysmal and whooping in pertussis [and asthma.]

It is needless to advert to the character of the *expectoration*, as that will at once command the attention of the practitioner. It may be *mucous, purulent, rusty, bloody and muco-purulent, nummular and heavy, putrid, etc., etc.*, each case giving its distinctive information of value to the examiner.

XVI.

MECHANICAL OR SURGICAL INJURY? Any wound, however trivial, makes its own demand on the powers of life. The amputation of an arm or limb, suggests inquiry as to the reason for the operation. Tuberculous deposit, malignant disease, caries and necrosis, requiring surgical interference, clearly invalidate the risk; whereas mere mechanical injuries, as causes, may not materially impair it. Caries, or even necrosis, from acute periostitis or external injury, even though ultimately requiring exsection or amputation, are, by no means, as serious objections to the risk as exostosis, enchondroma, osteo-sarcoma, cachectic deposit and the like. Statistics are wanting upon this point, but the writer's general judgment, from reading and observation, is, that the so-called capital operations, although recovered from, apparently, to a certain extent impair the desirability of the risk. Individual cases, it is true, may lend color to a different opinion, yet the stern proposition remains, that great injuries to the system, whether accidental or surgical, tend largely to exhaust the original powers of life and, *pro tanto*, impair the insurance expectation. In the case where a limb has been amputated after a long continued discharge, which has become habitual, although exhausting to the system, this remark is especially of importance. Apoplexies, paralyses and various organic affections are not unlikely to supervene. The old ulcer "cured," may involve new and unexpected disease. *Any* serious mechanical or surgical injury, *unexplained* — with no *positive* evidences to the contrary lessens the desirability of the risk. Long continued confinement in the recumbent position, of itself, predisposes to disease; and indeed any injury, which, although not severe in itself, has necessitated sedentary habits, with deficient air, exercise, etc., will leave traces of its deleterious influence on special organs or the general system.

XVII.

SEVERE PERSONAL INJURY OR DISEASE WITHIN THE LAST SEVEN YEARS? This query is based on the general idea that if more than seven years have elapsed the results of previous disease are little liable to be developed The popular opinion founded, as usual, upon an antique professional idea, is that the whole body is changed in its constitution every *seven* years. The instructed examiner needs not to be informed that all the moving and acting parts are changed in constitution within a space of time scarcely exceeding, if reaching, the third of a year. The practical rule, however, remains, recent diseases require more careful scrutiny as to their results than those which occurred long previous. Some companies under this head require details as to the character of the disease, and a reference to the attending physician. The latter point will be alluded to further along in this essay. The former will suggest, at once, to the intelligent examiner, the vast differences of degree and danger, of immediate or remote disastrous consequences, which may obtain in diseases which, for nosological purposes, receive the same name. Whatever the name, the practical fact remains that no disease is the product of a single cause, and varying with the multiplicity of influences acting upon different persons—will be the result, immediate or remote, of any single cause which may give the present affection its scientific appellation. Some organizations sustain and oppose the specific causes of certain diseases with little derangement even of functional action — others manifest the evidences — the gravest evidences, of organic and perhaps ultimately fatal change.

XVIII.

LONGEVITY OF ANCESTORS? In the United States, such is the character of the population, this question can, in the majority of instances, be answered only with reference to the grandparents. Yet the traditions of families, in the absence of registration statistics are worth something. The descendants of certain families are notably long-lived, and of others short-lived. Coincident with this fact will be found certain hereditary tendencies to disease. The family record, if tolerably complete and reliable, is of the highest insurance importance. It is well known that hereditary diseases not infrequently pass over one generation to appear in the next, or subsequent generations. The shape, capacity, and mode of action of internal organs are determined by the parentage, with as much constancy as the external likeness. These likenesses determine particular proclivities to intimate textural change, with the results of such change. Nations and tribes, clans and families have their marked peculiarities of external likeness, with almost identical tendencies toward death. This is especially true in the older countries, where rank, *caste*, and custom keep up the usage of intermarriage. It is of perhaps less importance in the United States, where these distinctions are only temporarily recognized. Nevertheless the observation of three generations, conduces much to correctness or judgement in any case under examination. If the grandparents on both paternal and maternal sides have reached old age the risk is more desirable. Longevity of grandparents on the maternal side is to be preferred to that on the paternal side. In either instance, if possible, the cause of the death of the grandparents should be noted. If either of them was affected by phthisis, or tuberculosis in any of its forms; by apoplexy or paralysis, by rheumatism or gout; by organic disease of the heart, Bright's disease, cancer, insanity or epilepsy; by syphilis, or other transmissible disease, the risk must be most carefully investigated. Meanwhile it should be recollected that change of location, intermarriage and habits, etc., are capable, under the guidance of the present developed principles of hygiene, of almost entirely controlling or obviating the hereditary tendency. All causes of disease thoroughly understood may, not only be robbed of their pernicious tendency but, be rendered subservient to the increased longevity of the race. It is to be recollected that progressive improvements in hygiene and medical science, as a whole, have largely increased the relative duration of human life, and that the longevity of our grandparents may, *cæteris paribus*, be well surpassed by this generation, and this still further increased by the next, by approximation to recognition of the great laws of health as now understood.

XIX.

Parents Living or Dead — PRESENT HEALTH OR CAUSE OF DEATH, RESPECTIVELY.— As previously remarked, hereditary predispositions require at least three generations for their satisfactory elucidation. But as one of these, and strongly influencing the result of observation, the peculiarities of parents should be studied. "When one only of the parents is the victim of constitutional disease, the tendency to similar constitutional diseases is most obviously expressed in those children who most resemble that parent in physical conformation and appearance, and it has been observed that, when both parents suffer, the tendency will sometimes be expressed more often in the daughters of the family than in the sons, or more often in the sons than in the daughters." The organic peculiarities, derived from the parent, will determine special and peculiar results from any accidental exciting cause.

But it should be recollected that the incidental occurrence of a family disease is less likely to be marked by acute, prolonged, or obstinate symptoms than when the same disease, nosologically, occurs in an individual without such hereditary predisposition. Nevertheless, its occurrence, whether severe or mild, fully determines the hereditary proclivity, and impairs the risk. Family proclivities to disease are more strikingly manifested in brothers and sisters than between parents and children. The intermingling of opposite tendencies begets, so to speak, in the children, a neutralization of the peculiar aptitudes to disease existing in the parents respectively. Physiological likeness of the parents induces imperfect progeny, *pro tanto*, just as certainly as intermarriage within the forbidden degrees of consanguinity. *En passant*, we remark, the offspring of cousins, etc., must be most carefully examined, prior to any recommendation of the risk. The question involving any such relationship of parents should never be omitted.

Tuberculosis, carcinoma, and other malignant formations, rheumatism, gout, insanity, paralysis, apoplexy, syphilitic, renal and cutaneous diseases, are especially noteworthy in this connection.

In considering the influence of hereditary tendency to disease, the remarks upon p. 6, *et seq.*, require attention. *It may have been outgrown, or not yet arrived at.* No sufficient exciting cause may have yet been presented. The individual may appear in high physical health, and yet be on the brink of disease of the most fatal kind.

It is fortunately the case that the medical science of the present time looks largely more to individual tendencies towards death, and suggests prophylactic hygienic measures, rather than engages in a wild pursuit of specifics and mysteriously operating agents, to do away with organic morbid changes already grown unmanageable and incurable.

The exact influence of hereditary tendency to dis ease can, probably, be never precisely estimated, because the vice of organization inherited will always increase the mortality from other forms. of disease The latent predisposition will manifest itself in that increased mortality. Nearly nine out of ten consumptive patients will be found, on investigation, to have lost one or two out of the immediate family connexion by phthisis.

A single instance in a family of a disease, usually hereditary, need not invalidate the risk. The party is thrown on his own personality. Both father and mother being of consumptive tendency, the risk should be declined. But either may have died of some accidental intercurrent disease or injury. Hence the personal peculiarities shonld be ascertained. The mother transmits disease more certainly than the father. But the likeness of organization, if it can be determined, affords the best method of general judgment. When, in addition to one, or both, of the parents, a brother or sister has died of an, usually, hereditary disease, the risk should be declined.

The author repeats his carefully considered and matured conviction, from the evidences, that brothers and sisters are more likely to manifest hereditary proclivities to disease than are parents and children. They inherit respectively the faults and virtues, as well physical as mental, of each of the parents. How far these may counteract each other, and produce a well balanced mental and physical organization, it is the duty of the Medical Examiner cautiously to consider.

In addition to general resemblance of external and internal organization, it should be recollected, members of the same family are likely to have acquired similarity of habits of living, diet, dress, exercise, exposure, etc., which cannot fail respectively to impress upon them similar tendencies to health or disease.

In this relation, also, it is well to bear in mind the physiological fact that half-brothers, or half-sisters, may indicate individual tendencies to organic change which may throw light on the constitutional peculiarities of the party under examination. The second husband may not solely be responsible for the organization of his own children. This point, it must be confessed, is one surrounded by obscurity, but the indefatigable medical agent of a life insurance society may derive, from the most unexpected quarters, evidences to guide him in forming an unexceptionable and reliable opinion.

XX.

Family Physician. — The Examiner should never neglect observance of this query. First, that he may have the testimony of the attendant medical man as to any peculiarities observed in previous diseases. Clear-headed medical men, in cases treated by them, gain cognizance, not only of present severe symptoms, but, what is of more importance, of the tendencies towards a particular form of death. Some physicians, and a great deal of cheap rhetoric has been expended upon this point, complain that insurance companies do not pay them for the information conveyed in their certificate. This is simply absurd. The family physician is the friend of the party applying, and, it is fair to presume, has relations with the party not altogether of the eleemosynary kind. The trouble of filling out the certificate is merely trivial, being altogether historical in its nature. Yet it is of value — not solely to the company. Doubtful points may be thereby explained, and difficulties cleared up. The professional character of the physician, it is needless to say, lends much of confidence to the examiner in making up his opinion. Aside from his certificate, his attendance upon the party may lessen (or increase) the dangers of accidental disease. One or two companies advertise a reduction of rates, even so much as *ten per cent.*, provided a particular species of family "physician" is employed. This would be startling to life companies, and examiners generally, were it not so clearly an advertising device — the expense to be defrayed by diminished dividends to the insured.

XXI.

Intimate Friend Referred to. — There may be circumstances affecting the prospects of longevity which the applicant is either ignorant of, or wilfully withholds. Thus, habits of intemperance are most frequently of all denied by the party himself, and these may be made known by his acquaintances. The solicitor ought not to neglect inquiry upon this point, and submit to the examiner the friend's certificate.

Again, the applicant may have had "fits"—epileptic or apoplectic seizure, etc., the real significance of which may, for prudential or other reasons, have been withheld from his knowledge. For these and similar reasons, the corroborative evidence thus gained, should be laid before the examiner.

XXII.

Previous Rejection or Assurance.— The fact of previous insurance should never be permitted to lessen the care of inspection. The previous examiner may have been inexpert or careless, or have inadvertently overlooked some important point. Or, again, acute or chronic, or even hereditary diseases, may have since been developed, involving organic changes of immediate or remote danger. *Previous rejection* demands employment of all the physician's skill in diagnosis. The real cause for such rejection should be discovered, if possible. It may have been in consequence of the applicant's then habits, and some other reason assigned to spare personal feeling. It may have been from some temporary ailment present, or not yet fully recovered from. It may have been from misapprehension of the applicant's answers on certain points, or from misinterpretation of symptoms observed. Or, again, because the company to which application was made, excluded a particular class of cases which other companies accept. Or, by the baldest hypothesis, it may have been from the human weakness of attempting to gain credit for remarkable professional skill and acumen, at a cheap rate.

But when the previous examiner and the attendant circumstances are fully known, nothing but positive demonstration will warrant the medical man in recommending the risk. It must be *demonstrated* that the previous disease is fully recovered from; that the hereditary taint is absent; that bad habits do not exist; that the heart or lungs, or other organ blamed, are respectively free from lesion. Whilst a needless rejection does permanent injustice to both the appiirant and the company, every medical examiner must avoid the imputation of making the company by whom he is engaged, a hospital for invalid risks.

XXIII.

Is the Applicant fully Aware OF THE PURPORT OF THE QUESTIONS HE HAS ANSWERED AND SUBSCRIBED? He may be of limited intelligence, or unfamiliar with the language, the names of the diseases alluded to, etc. The solicitor may have been careless in his method, and thus periled the party's subsequent rights, as well as tending to mislead the examiner.

Wherever there is the slightest cause to apprenend any negligence or mistake in this matter, the examiner should himself again propound the necessary questions.

THE EXAMINATION.

In order that no point may be overlooked, the Medical Examiner should adopt a regular method of personal examination of the applicant — the form adopted by the company for which he acts being carefully adhered to, but, nevertheless, considered merely as suggestive, not exhaustive. All the considerations noticed in the Applicant's personal history, must be given full weight in the proposition of further questions, and still more careful observation. Although not in accordance with the usual mode of systematic *general* diagnosis, the purposes of this essay will, perhaps, be better subserved by adhering to the more generally adopted formulæ furnished by the insurance companies.

Be sure that the person examined is the one whose application has been read over. Mistakes here occasionally occur, especially when parties have the same names, or several applications are received at once. These blunders might be deemed merely ludicrous, were they not so important in their probable results.

I.

Height and Weight.—Whilst the general proportions are, perhaps, of the most importance, yet the rule is, that the medium height is endowed with the greatest endurance. Five feet and eight inches may be taken as the medium in this country, for adult males. The average of adult females is, of course considerably below this—but statistics are wanting upon the subject. Probably five feet and one and a half inches is the approximately correct standard. Emigrants from Continental Europe average a little less than five feet six inches, if we except certain races, as the Hungarians, Poles, and Sclaves, who reach the American standard. Emigrants from the British Islands average about five feet seven inches.

In this country, the average height of persons bred and living in large towns and cities, is something less than that of those living in rural districts, whilst in Europe, the reverse is claimed to be the case. This fact is important, as to a certain extent indicating the general hygienic influences which have operated on races, families, and, ultimately, the individual. The better developed having been from a better nourished stock, and physically superior lineage.

Very tall men are usually of less muscular power, less respiratory activity, with a greater tendency to cardiac and pulmonary diseases. They are more liable to hernia, varicose veins, and ulcers of an obstinate kind upon the extremities. Acute diseases attacking them are more disposed to assume the chronic form, with general breaking down of the constitution. On the other hand, short persons are apt to be disproportionately developed; their muscular power, and capacity for physical endurance are small, and they become the ready victims of acute, and especially epidemic diseases.

The relation of age to the height ahould never be overlooked, but this will be alluded to a little further along

THE WEIGHT is of moment, relatively to the height. The simplest statement of the due relation is that of Dr. Brinton: "As a rule, it may be laid down that an adult male, in good health, 66 inches in stature, ought to weigh rather more than ten stones, or 140 pounds avoirdupois. And for every inch above and below this height, we may respectively add and subtract about five pounds."

Individuals may present a wide range of variation from this; "But as a rule, twenty per cent., or one-fifth, is almost the maximum variation within the limits of health."

The annexed table is introduced for convenience of reference :

HEIGHT.	WEIGHT.	MEDIUM CHEST.
5 feet 1 inch	Should weigh 120 lbs	34.06 inch.
5 " 2 "	" " 125 "	35.13 "
5 " 3 "	" " 130 "	35.70 "
5 " 4 "	" " 135 "	36.26 "
5 " 5 "	" " 140 "	36.83 "
5 " 6 "	" " 143 "	37.50 "
5 " 7 "	" " 145 "	38.16 "
5 " 8 "	" " 148 "	38.53 "
5 " 9 "	" " 155 "	39.10 "
5 " 10 "	" " 160 "	39.66 "
5 " 11 "	" " 165 "	40.23 "
6 "	" " 170 "	40.80 "

The maximum of height is usually reached at twenty-five — the rate of progress being about ten inches from eleven to eighteen, and two inches only from that age to maturity. An increment much surpassing this during the latter epoch is a suspicious circumstance, and unless accompanied by apparent coincident development of the nutrient energy, and correspondent increase of weight, impairs the risk.

Excessive obesity at any period vitiates the risk, and particularly where it has come on within a comparatively brief period. After the age of complete maturity, usually, there is a deposit of adipose tissue which largely increases the relative proportion of the weight to the height; and if this occurs gradually and if clearly traceable to hereditary peculiarity it does not disparage the risk. But the rapid occurrence of corpulence points almost infallibly to deterioration of nutrition, the result of, it may be, newly formed sedentary habits, intemperance, internal organic disease, or that general cachexia which accompanies fatty degenerations.

On the other hand emaciation slow and progressive after middle life, if *clearly* a family characteristic does not necessarily disqualify, although it demands close investigation. Rapid emaciation, even without apparent organic cause, rejects.

Incidentally it may be remarked, that measurement of the chest will afford an index of the relative proportions of the height and weight. The rule suggested by Brent is sufficiently exact. Measured over the nipples :

Minimum chest: half of the stature, minus one-sixty-first of the stature, is equal to circumference of the chest.

Medium chest: half of the stature, plus one-fifteenth of the stature, is equal to circumference of the chest.

Maximum chest: two-thirds of the stature is equal to circumference of the chest.

Irrespective of the height, the general statement is authorized that "the circumference of the chest increases exactly one inch for every ten pounds increase of weight."

If these proportions are widely departed from, the case requires research as to the cause of the unusual deposit.

So, also, local emaciation suggests similar caution. Incipient phthisis generally is denoted by wasting of the tissues of the thorax and of the arms, long before it is to be observed in the face or lower extremities.

At the present time, when a large proportion of the adult males wishing to be insured have recently returned from the exposures of army life, it is well to bear in mind that diminished weight is one of the most significant evidences of chronic, and possibly, painless diarhœa.

II.

General Appearance. — The proportionate height and weight with the more or less symmetrical development of the body, as a whole, make up a part of the general appearance; but beyond this the attention of the examiner is to be directed to various details which go to make up the *tout ensemble*. Among these we specify: *Aspect of the Countenance, Complexion, Color of the Hair and Eyes, Size of the Bones, Contour of Muscles, Gait, Apparent Age, Temperament, Idiosyncrasy.*

ASPECT OF COUNTENANCE.—Experienced observers readily recognize in diseases a physiognomy peculiar to each, always difficult and often impossible satisfactorily to describe, nevertheless so distinguishable as to be worthy of serious consideration in judging of a risk. By this observation they can ultimately decide, almost as quickly as an expert cashier upon the genuineness of a signature or bank note. But this acquired skill and readiness never, when such large interests are in issue, should be relied upon to the exclusion of those rigid tests by which the *opinion* may be solidified into an unassailable judgment. We notice here a few only of the more striking facts, as indicating the direction of observation.

The aspect may inform of tuberculous cachexia by the delicate skin, tumid upper lip, long eyelashes, pearly conjunctiva, etc. Or it may denote the cancerous diathesis by its sallow anæmic hue intermingled with muscular markings, indicating frequently recurring or continuous pain, or of that organic pain of which consciousness as yet takes no note, but which equally calls into action the reflex sympathies of the nervous apparatus.

Hepatic disease, with its more or less yellow tinge and hypochondriacal look. Or renal affection, with its puffy eyelids, sodden or waxy skin, and features either downcast or stolid and apathetic.

Hypertrophy of the heart, with its unnatural fulness and congestion, or the same look from habitual intemperance. Or the facial muscles may be permanently contracted in forms which indicate the continuous suffering of wasting local or general disease. Lesions affecting the nervous centres may find here their earliest exponent. The countenance, which tranquil shows no disorder, when wakened by movement may give warning of coming paralysis. Or the furtive glance from the eyes, notwithstanding immobility of the other features, may warn of impending insanity. Or the rapid transitions in expression, flashing or wandering and unsteady eyes may indicate a different form of the same malady. Or the whole face may be dull and listless, the eye sluggish, and the physiognomy of softening of the brain be almost beyond mistake.

COMPLEXION. — This should be noticed as going to make up the temperament hereafter to be considered. But any peculiarities in hue which it may have derived from antecedent or present disease or exposure should be noted, whether rendered sallow by residence in malarious districts, bronzed by exposure or Addison's disease, unnaturally florid by intemperance or cardiac lesion, livid by imperfect aeration of the blood from whatever cause, or "compounded of alabaster and the rose" by incipient phthisis, or pallid and sodden from albuminuria and anæmia.

COLOR OF THE HAIR AND EYES. — This point also refers particularly to the temperament; but attention is called here to changes in the color of the hair from advancing or premature age; to its nutrition, whether dry and husky or soft and silken in texture — whether it remains firmly rooted or has fallen. These observations may give a clue to the diathesis or cachexia present.

The movements of the eye, its expression, the condition of the pupil, contracted or dilated, or whether these changes are symmetrical; whether there be complete or partial amaurosis of either; the *arcus senilis*, etc.

It will be found that the eyes can afford vastly more information than merely as to their color.

SIZE OF THE BONES.— A strong bony framework is usually connected with strength of the nutrient system, and is indicative of a constitution capable of much endurance. Prominence of the apophyses is an index, generally, of a fully developed muscular system with its concurrent advantages. But reference to the osseous system involves more than simple observation of the size of the bones and their normal projections. It suggests inquiry into the perfection of ossification about the cranium and vertebral column, original or acquired deformity, *rachitis*, *mollities ossium*, curvatures of the spine, gibbosity, &c., fragility, caries, necrosis, morbid growths, etc.

CONTOUR OF MUSCLES.— Closely allied in prognostic meaning to the development of the bones, will be found the firmness and abundance of the muscular fibre. The deposit of adipose tissue will often obscure the strong lines which mark the boundaries of the muscles, but their compact structure, contractility and tonicity can readily be observed. The well rounded and well developed muscular system renders the risk more desirable, as the feeble, ill developed fibre suggests the reverse.

Attention is here directed to local paralysis, which may be present as the result of lead or other poisoning, central or excentric affections of the nervous system, &c. Or again, tonic or clonic spasms, tremors, tremulousness, chorea, &c.

APPARENT AGE.— The applicant having recorded his age, it is proper to compare his apparent with his actual age. Some are really older at forty than others at sixty. Premature old age may be from hereditary or congenital imperfection of structure, or it may be the evidence of previous sickness, long continued ill health, irregular or dissipated habits, overwork, exposure and the like. As a general rule, when the applicant is really older than he looks to be, his life expectation surpasses the average; but when he has aged beyond his years, the risk is thereby in so far impaired.

TEMPERAMENT.— In noting the temperament it is better to adopt the simplest possible varieties, recollecting that the phrase is employed simply to express the preponderance in activity of certain organs or apparatuses in the individual. Practically *four* temperaments may be recognized for purposes of description. the *Sanguine, Bilious or Sarcous, Phlegmatic or Lymphatic,* and the *Nervous.*

The *Sanguine* temperament is characterized by great activity of the blood making organs, rapid integral changes and free excretion. Activity of mental and muscular movements, delicacy of the skin, etc., are incidental to these. Light or sandy hair, blue eyes, florid complexion and the like are accidental, not necessary concomitants, being frequently conjoined with the other temperaments.

The *Phlegmatic* temperament shows, nearly an opposite condition of the organism. There is slow and imperfect nutrition—the blood tardily developed and assimilation comparatively feeble. Hence languor of both mind and muscle, infrequent and compressible pulse, flabby and soft texture, with abundant adipose deposit.

The *Bilious* temperament is characterized by great perfection of assimilation, but not remarkable energy of digestion. The blood making processes are not as active as in the sanguine, because there is less of waste. The quantity of *excreta* is also less. Firmness and strength of muscle characteristically predominate. The less rapidly changing skin assumes a darker hue, and with its appendages, hair, nails, &c., is drier and harsher. Coincidently the liver and subsidiary organs are largely taxed, for the recomposition of blood deficiently renewed by food.

The *Nervous* temperament, with deficient digestive energy and muscular development, manifests a striking activity of the so called nervous processes. "The countenance is usually pale and the features thin and sharp, the pulse is quick, small and frequent; the respiration active; the chest not largely developed; the skin dry and rough." These are the incidents of the organic peculiarities before noted.

Each of these temperaments, it is of course understood, may be modified in its manifestations by a combination with one of the others—a result not unlikely to occur when the parents have been of dissimilar temperaments. But almost typical specimens are afforded by families, and even tribes or races, when intermarriage has been restricted within narrow limits. In this country where individuals of the most diverse nationality and parentage are "marrying and giving in marriage," it is constantly becoming more difficult to assign the proper status in this regard. The point to be kept in mind is, not the accidents of color, shape, &c., but the preponderant activity of special organs and processes. Thus the child always approximates the sanguine; the adult, at maturity, the sarcous, and in the decline of life lapses into the nervous or phlegmatic, according to the peculiar organization.

Relative to life assurance, the matter becomes of importance, as evincing proclivities to particular forms of disease. This is noteworthy when there exists any hereditary or acquired predisposition thereto, or when the occupation, habits, residence, &c., renders the party liable to the usual exciting causes. The sanguine temperament predisposes to miasmatic diseases, typhoid and remittent fevers, the exanthems, to acute rheumatism, organic and functional diseases of the heart and arteries, to hæmorhages and under conditions unfavorable to nutrition to tuberculosis.

The phlegmatic temperament on the contrary predisposes to chronic and often incurable inflammations, dropsies and fluxes of various kinds, especially from mucous membranes, influenza and scrofulosis.

The bilious temperament favors the occurrence of endemic disease, febrile affections tending to a low grade, hepatic obstruction with dysentery, hæmorrhoids, *fistula in ano.* &c. When rheumatism occurs in this organization the heart rarely escapes being involved sooner or later.

The nervous temperament involves liability to insanity, epilepsy, paralysis and neuroses generally. If typhoid fever happens to such an one the issue is very dangerous.

In taking note of the GENERAL APPEARANCE any IDIOSYNCRASY present deserves careful attention and its possible bearing upon the life prospects of the party must be noted. Idiosyncrasies vary so remarkably in their characters that it is unnecessary to do more than simply direct notice to the fact that they are capable cf largely modifying particular indications, and indeed the ultimate judgment.

II.

The Pulse demands attention to its frequency, rhythm and general character. Indications derived from it require analysis to be at all satisfactory.

The normal pulse described by authors for the adult male ranges in frequency from sixty-eight to seventy-two; more frequent in infancy, childhood and youth—again rising in frequency in advanced age, although gradually diminishing from maturity to perhaps sixty or seventy. It is slower in the morning than in the evening. It is more frequent in the erect position than when sitting, and still less rapid when recumbent. It is hastened by nervous excitement or muscular exercise. Any tension of the contractile fibre will easily cause it to rise from the usual standard to even double its ordinary rate. In fine it is rather an index of the nervous system than, as formerly supposed, of circulatory energy.

The pulse of Great Britain and Continental Europe ranges from sixty-eight to seventy-two, but that of the Atlantic States of America from seventy-two to seventy-six, while that of the Northwest will rarely be less than seventy-six to eighty. A pulse uniformly, or even temporarily, below sixty or above ninety must be explained by idiosyncrasy, or else it rejects—at the best postpones judgement.

The irregular pulse must be likewise demonstrated to be an individual characteristic; otherwise it rejects. Unexplained it is totally exclusive.

The intermittent pulse calls attention to probable cerebral or cardiac disease. Occasionally it is the result of temporary gastric or other local disorder; but even then it should cause suspension of judgment. The rate of the pulse should be recorded when the applicant is sitting, or, better, the difference in rate between the two positions should be given.

The hammering pulse emphatically calls attention to the cardiac valves.

The general character of the pulse is expressed by the terms full, free, hard, soft, weak, etc.

While considering the pulse the whole arterial system should be taken under review. Unnatural or extraordinary hardness possibly indicative of senile or calcareous degeneration of the arterial parietes, to ultimate in aneurism, senile gangrene or embolism.

But the pulse is *fallacissima rerum*

III.

The Respiratory Organs.— A fully developed and powerful thorax is one of the best evidences of general physical capacity and endurance, whilst a narrow, contracted or malformed chest is a strong evidence of a feeble constitution. The methods of investigation differ somewhat in details, but all coincide in essentials.

MENSURATION.—Some details have already been given (p. 56 *et seq.*,)as to the relation of the circumference of the chest to the height and weight. It is well to bear in mind that due proportion requires that the circumference should equal twice the distance between the angles of the shoulders; that it should be four times the antero-posterior diameter at the lower portion of the sternum, and that this latter diameter should exactly equal the distance between the nipples.

Practically, measurement is best made with the simple graduated tape line, which adapts itself readily to the surface and can be always carried in the pocket. For physiological investigations other instruments may be of service, but are unnecessary here. The line should be applied under the vest, if practicable, at the level of the nipples, and on the same plane anteriorly and posteriorly. If taken over the vest, or there is much clothing beneath the tape, a suitable allowance must be made therefor.

Note now the measurement:

1st. During the largest inspiration.

2d. During forced expiration.

3d. During tranquil respiration about the middle of inspiration.

The first and second measurements give a clue to the capacity of the lungs for the "complemental" air or extreme *vital capacity*, whilst the third suggests the amount of "tidal" or ordinary breathing air, which is perhaps of equal importance, as exhibiting the individual's present condition. A man five feet eight inches should have a breathing capacity of 230 cubic inches of air, while in point of fact, in tranquil respiration there is not usually a change of over 20 or 30 cubic inches within the lungs. Nevertheless the physical capacity for large aeration of the blood adds to the desirability of the risk.

The extreme breathing capacity is increased eight cubic inches for every additional inch of stature between five and six feet, when due proportion is maintained. If this proportion is not maintained the risk is, in so far, impaired.

Observations made with the spirometer, although interesting in a physiological point of view, are practically of no avail to the insurance examiner. Incidentally it may be observed that the extreme breathing capacity is diminished by obesity; that it is proportionately less in females than in males, and in children than in adults. The volume increases with age to the thirtieth year, and gradually decreases from thence to the decline of life. A deficiency from the normal standard of sixteen per cent. is suspicious, and if very much below this will invalidate the risk. Coincident signs or symptoms under such circumstances, will almost invariably confirm indications on this point.

The average expansion in full respiration will be found to be a little over three inches, but in tranquil respiration it is scarcely more than an inch. The right side expands a little more than the left, as it is generally, in right handed persons, a little over half an inch largest. Any variation from the normal amount of expansion at any part of the chest should be noted, and its cause sought out.

INSPECTION.— The general form of the chest will suggest particular observation. Thus, whether there be any flattening, especially in the clavicular regions, or even across the whole anterior surface, with stooping shoulders, curved sternum and projecting inferior angles of the scapulæ — collectively indicative of feebleness of constitution, slight power of endurance, and proneness to tubercular deposit.

Flattening of the lateral or inferior portions, significant of old pleurisy with remaining adhesion, or of old abscesses, &c.

Again, deficient transverse diameter with projection of the sternum, or "chicken-breast," suggestive of causes of dyspnœa in early life, or perhaps now present, or again, of *rachitis*, &c. The chicken-breast is ordinarily indicative of deficient vital capacity, and although not seemingly productive of inconvenience, may, nevertheless, like "hunchback," militate against the risk.

RESPIRATORY MOVEMENTS.—The frequency, rhythm and type of motion in inspiration and expiration are to be noted.

In the adult male, during tranquil breathing, the average frequency of inspiration may be placed at from fifteen to twenty per minute, or about 17, but the slightest mental influences or exercise will vary this widely. Probably the point of most importance is *the ratio to the pulse*, which should be very closely as one to four or five. The movements should be noted while numbering the pulse, and the ratio then observed. Nevertheless, as a rule, if the respiratory acts are less frequent than twelve or more than twenty-four, decision should be suspended. It is to be recollected, as Walshe observes, that the rapidity, energy and extent of these movements "increase in the direct ratio of the easy mobility' of the framework of the chest (hence greater in youth than age,) and the height of the individual." In females, generally, and in males of a nervous temperament, the frequency is exaggerated easily, and, as a rule, slowness of these movements is a more objectionable feature than its opposite. But coincident evidence will usually explain satisfactorily the cause.

The fifth expiration (on the average,) is a little deeper than the others. The ratio of inspiration, expiration and quiescence should be about as five, four and one respectively.

If the motions are irregular, intermittent or jerking, the case requires scrutiny. If the ratio is widely departed from, further investigation is demanded, particularly where expiration is prolonged—the latter symptoms awakening great anxiety. The irregular, intermittent or jerking respiration is usually indicative of derangement of the nervous system, but prolonged expiration minatory of local lesion of the lungs. It may become more than twice the length of the inspiration.

The *type* should be abdominal in the infant, diaphragmatic and inferior costal in the adult male; superior costal in the adult female. Any change of these types is suspicious. Notably so pectoral breathing of marked character in the man, and even in the woman, when exaggerated and accompanied by a perperceptible rising of the shoulders with each inspiration.

DISEASES.— Acute diseases of the respiratory organs postpone and, after apparent cure, demand search for lesions left behind. Catarrh, Pharyngitis, Laryngitis, Tracheitis and Bronchitis do not necessarily involve a tendency to Phthisis Pulmonalis, but their frequent recurrence gives grave doubts, which must be cleared up before insurance. If they assume the chronic form, it becomes imperative to demonstrate the absence of the tuberculous taint. Or perhaps they may be the sole exponents of Syphilis or other cachexia.

Ulceration of the larynx is about infallibly an evidence of tuberculosis or syphilis.

A slight catarrhal condition of the respiratory mucous membrane may have become habitual, and in the assured absence of any constitutional cachexia, or hereditary tendency, need not preclude the risk, although placing it in lower grade.

But the attention of the Examiner is with greater earnestness called to the more prominent affections which, when decided to be present, must necessarily induce him to decline the risk.

As this is not intended as a systematic treatise on nosology or diagnosis, for convenience I shall consider these affections in alphabetical order.

ADHESIONS of the pleural surfaces often occur without noticeable morbific results. It is important to recognize the condition so as not to confound such signs as it may afford with those of a graver character. They impair the mobility of the parietes, and occasionally that of the arm of the affected side. Flattening or contraction, more or less discernible, usually of the lower and lateral parts of the chest; feeble respiration; very slight diminution of resonance; no bronchophony or augmented vocal fremitus; interrupted respiration, but not prolonged expiration Diagnosis will be materally assisted by noting historical symptoms and absence of tuberculous diathesis. Unless the pleurisy has become chronic, or the adhesion is so extensive as to materially impair the breathing capacity, this condition need not necessarily reject, but assigns to a lower grade. When the results are seen at the superior portion of the lobes, its almost certain coincidence with tuberculous deposit and resulting inflammation, necessitates rejection.

ASTHMA has already been noticed, (p. 17, *et seq*,) but when the party has wilfully or negligently concealed its previous occurrence, it may often be detected by its peculiar dry wheezing or sibilant whistle, even during the interim. The affections upon which it may depend or with wnich it may be confounded will be considered in another place. See, also, p. 18 *et seq*.

APHONIA may be due to nervous disorder, as hysteria or hypochondria; or it may evidence organic lesion of the nervous centre; or local paralysis from loca causes only; a turgid state of the laryngeal surfaces; or ulceration, or, in old age, ossification of the cartilages. It is an occasional result of rheumatism, and in some instances arises from the pressure of a dilated or aneurismal aorta or other tumor.

When present it must be demonstrated to depend on the trivial and transitory, and not upon the graver causes. Its intimate relation with tubercular phthisis and syphilis renders it deserving of analysis.

CONGESTION.—It occasionally occurs, on percussion, that there is evident diminution of the normal resonance, with deficient respiratory sound on auscultation, at the same time, the pitch is slightly elevated. The ratio of inspiration to expiration may be unchanged —the movements slightly augmented in frequency, and a trifle more of muscular effort observable, without marked dyspnœa being present. With the feeble respiration there may sometimes be noticed a "dryish, rather fine, but distinctly bubbling rhonchus."

This condition may be only temporary or be permanent in its character, as dependent on its cause. It is important to diagnose it from tuberculous or other deposits. It is the result of congestion, and, possibly, also slight pulmonary œdema. It demands research for the obstruction.

It is capable of being brought on, temporarily, by the ordinary viscissitudes of temperature and humidity, "functional" diseases of the heart, liver, nervous apparatus, &c.; or, by special influences—malaria, gaseous or atomic emanations, retained excreta and the like.

But it is also often the result of more or less permanent obstruction in the pulmonary blood-vessels, or, again, the heart. When present it should postpone decision until after a subsequent examination. Or else, if the organic origin be determined, cause immediate rejection. But it is due the applicant not to confound it with the result of tuberculous deposit, or other grave disease.

DYSPNŒA—depends upon such a variety of causes that it is not diagnostic, alone, of any single disease. When considerable and permanent it should reject, whatever the apparent cause. It may, however, be but a peculiarity of a nervous temperament, or originated only occasionally by peculiar influences depending on idiosyncrasy.

If caused by permanent obstruction to the diaphragmatic movements, or by disease of the larynx, trachea, lung tissue, pleura or heart—it must reject, at least while present. It is well to recollect, that it is rarely a concomitant of tuberculous deposit; hence, the popular notion that phthisis and "asthma" are incompatible.

DEPOSITS—may be of great variety. Prominently may be noticed: the *Inflammatory, Tuberculous, Cancerous, Melanoid, Typhoid, and Syphilitic*. The first two only claim particular notice in this place, as any peculiarities about the latter four will be found to depend on the diathesis or cachexia by which they are to be determined.

The results of *Inflammatory deposit* in the parenchyma are traceable from historical and present symptoms, and the physical signs.

The consolidated exudate of acute pneumonia may remain unabsorbed a long time, or even permanently after the individual has regained apparent health. Contracting, as does all inflammatory exudate, the side of the chest overlying may flatten as after pleurisy. There is less range of costal motion resulting (p. 71). It is dull on percussion, with bronchial respiration and broncophony over the affected part of the lobe—not even feeble respiration being heard as after pleurisy. Occasionally around the part there is uneven, feeble respiration, but this is rather significant of œdema of the parenchyma, as, otherwise, it will be found harsher or puerile. Combined with these signs it will be found, on cautious inquiry, that there are dyspepsia and irregular febrile accessions—none of which may be of sufficient severity to attract attention unless sought for.

This deposit temporarily postpones—but its diagnosis from tuberculous deposit should be made out, if possible, to give opportunity for subsequent examination—as well as in case of cure to protect the Examiner's own reputation. All the evidences of the tuberculous diathesis must be explored; for, even when the physical signs presented are not about the apices, it is well to bear in mind that there may occur tuberculous degeneration of the exudate. Where it involves the apices, the diathesis, hereditary, or acquired, affords our only means of judging of the abnormal material present.

The Life Insurance Examiner is not called upon by Companies to investigate well marked cases of *Tuberculous Deposit*, accompanied with its well known rational symptoms. He is to watch for its incipiency with the extremest anxiety, for it is known to be the greatest possible source of their financial losses. *Obsta principiis* is, most emphatically, to be his motto. By his exercise of care, skill and sagacity he will be enabled to reduce those losses to a minimum unexpected before the introduction of Physical Diagnosis.

It is proper to remark, that when the physical signs give evidence of deposit about the superior lobes of the lungs it must reject, whatever the apparent diathesis. It is equally important to remember that the diathesis may be strongly marked—to such an extent, indeed as to determine rejection, when none of the usual signs of deposit are discoverable. In the vast majority of cases, the two are associated long before manifestation of any of the characteristic symptoms produced by the process of softening.

Perhaps the most observable early sign is *Prolonged Expiration;* then *Vesicular Murmur* lessened at the part —*Puerile* around; *Inspiratory Sound* less forcible, higher in pitch, and *Bronchial Respiration* more distinctly tubular; *Vocal Fremitus* exaggerated; *Dullness* more or less decided on Percussion ; a little later, *Flattening* with less superior costal motion and more diaphragmatic—the shoulders being more perceptibly elevated at each inspiration, whilst the general frequency of the movements is accelerated to 24 or 28 in the minute, or even beyond this on the slightest excitement.

Owing, probably, to their usually more quiescent state, the apices of the lungs are most liable to the deposit, but other causes enforcing similar quiescence of any part of the parenchyma may determine its location in that part. The *supra scapular*, *supra*, and *infra clavicular* regions, in the absence of historical symptoms pointing elsewhere, are the parts first to come under investigation.

In these regions *percussion sound* elicited may be deficient in clearness and in duration, with lessened elasticity, and even when the deposit is small and in scattered points, there will be less increase in resonance over the affected than the sound part, when the lung is inflated by full inspiration—the dullness more pronounced at the end of a complete expiration.

By *auscultation* the vesicular sounds may be found varied within a limited space—suppressed, weak or exaggerated. The displaced tubular sound elevated in pitch, harsher and prolonged. Crepitant dry rales, or, later, of a moist character. More or less distinct broncophony, and the sounds of the heart heard with unusual distinctness through the changed conducting medium. The rhythm, as previously noted, is liable to irregularity.

The physical signs thus briefly alluded to determine the presence of an abnormal deposit more or less extensive, according to their distinctness of manifestation, and, even in the absence of the so-called 'rational symptoms' of incipient Phthisis, preclude insurance—*unqualifiedly*.

Not all of them may be present, and doubt may arise, to be decided perhaps by reference to the history and diathesis of the applicant. If these are unsatisfactory, the company must have the benefit of the doubt and the party be declined. (Vid. DIATHESIS.)

The *Typhoid Deposit* is noticeable for the reason that whereas it will yield the same physical signs as the true tubercular, and is prone to produce similar results by its softening, nevertheless it is capable often of being permanently removed, and perfect local and constitutional health be restored; so that the case once properly rejected by an experienced examiner may, ultimately, be accepted by one equally as cautious and expert.

The same remark may be made with regard to the *Syphilitic Deposit*. The "gummata' will yield the same physical signs as tubercle, but eventually, under appropriate treatment, disappear. But while present they reject—as must the cachexia upon which they depend.

The *Cancerous* and *Melanoid Deposits* likewise exclude, because of the physical signs afforded, as well as the cachexiæ originating them.

EMPHYSEMA.— The pathological and prognostic importance of this lesion depends wholly upon its causation. Unless very extensive it may not be said to shorten life, yet, like a contracted chest and small lungs, it lessens vital capacity for aerating the blood under circumstances demanding an increase of the usual energy of the process, and thus renders its subject an easier prey to intercurrent diseases. A local Emphysematous condition is not infrequently associated with tubercular lesion, but ordinarily its presence over any considerable portion of the parenchyma is said to lessen the liability to tubercle, hæmoptysis and pneumonia. Hypertrophous Emphysema is a nearly incurable affection—the Atrophous or Senile form absolutely so. Both varieties tend to produce enlargement of the heart. The hypertrophous form is usually associated with and probably caused by bronchitis, which therefore should be looked for. It may be hereditary, and in its manifestation is confined to no age, sex, or condition. The atrophous form is confined mainly to those well advanced in years. In the first form the chest is locally or generally enlarged, so as to give a bulging appearance, very peculiar in character when considerable in extent. The spine curves anteriorly, and the angle of junction with the ribs becomes more obtuse.

Percussion gives increased resonance, sometimes of drum-like intensity, but with lesssened resistance of the thoracic parietes. Auscultation shows feeble respiration in the affected parts with, it may be, puerile or harsh vesicular murmur in the healthy structure. Associated with these are usually found the abnormal sounds of bronchitis or asthma. The rhythm of the inspiratory movements is likely to be irregular, and expiration prolonged.

There is dyspnœa continually, and this, at times, deepens into the asthmatic paroxysm. The superficial veins are turgescent, and the hue of the skin is darkened by the imperfectly aerated blood. The features wear the characteristic marks of habitual laborious breathing. With exception of the general expansion and bulging of the chest, the atrophous variety presents a similar array of signs and symptoms. The existence of either form of the lesion being established, the applicant must be rejected.

EMPYÆMIA is usually made out with sufficient accuracy by the historic and present symptoms, and the physical signs of pleuritic effusion. It of course rejects. It may be borne in mind that occasionally a fistulous opening occurs, and the contentsof the pleural cavity are discharged a long distance from it. Such cases, with tolerably fair health, have been mistaken for fistulæ or ulcers from other causes. The previous occurrence of pleurisy and the presence of a supposed "fever sore" on the back or elsewhere that pus may find its way, demands caution.

HÆMOPTYSIS has been referred to (p. 34).

HÆMATEMESIS.—(Vid. p. 35.)

HYDROTHORAX — although the party may appear otherwise in perfect health, while present postpones, whatever the cause. If connected with structural lesion of the heart, liver or kidneys, it positively declines.

PNEUMOTHORAX rejects as decidedly as Emphysema, and hence its differential diagnosis from the latter is unnecessary.

PLEURODYNIA, being but a mere symptom, requires analysis. The term is carelessly applied to cases which may prove to be rheumatism of the intercostal muscles; intercostal neuralgia, the chest pains of phthisis, or chronic pleurisy, or from carcinoma within the parietes. It is properly restricted to the first mentioned disorder. The pain on movement is likely to locally diminish the expansion of the parietes, and hence there will be less distinct respiratory murmur, and less resonance on percussion. The remarkable aggravation of pain by movement, absence of other physical signs of deposit, &c., and reference to the diathesis, will be sufficient to diagnose the case.

Intercostal neuralgia is distinguishable by the absence of abnormal physical signs—by its tendency to paroxysmal or periodical forms, and by the diathesis present. Its obstinate continuance may point to spinal lesion, or that of remote organs with which the part affected is in relation through reflex nervous action. Movements aggravate it very little if at all. Neither the simple rheumatic or neuralgic affection rejects, unless connected with evidence of constitutional or organic disease.

The chest pains of phthisis, chronic pleurisy, carcinoma, &c., need only be mentioned to direct the attention of the examiner to their differential diagnosis Of course each rejects.

TUMORS, within the thoracic cavities, whatever their nature, may attain considerable size before producing noticeable symptoms. Eventually their pressure upon the lungs or heart, the nerves or blood-vessels may give rise to pain, dyspnœa, palpitation, dysphagia, displacement of organs, interference with the circulation, hæmoptysis, inflammation with its results, bulging of the ribs and sternum, &c. But where these symptoms are present parties rarely present themselves for examination, or if they do, the matter is easily disposed of.

According to their location they will change the normal auscultatory and percussion sounds. Diminished resonance and feeble vesicular murmur are the necessary physical signs. Light percussion may show resonance, whilst a stronger blow will elicit deep-seated dullness. The particular character of the tumor can only be surmised from concurrent symptoms, and the diathesis or cachexia present. The most satisfactory diagnosis is here the result of the *exclusive* metnod—determining the absence of other lesions which might account for the signs and symptoms.

The intra-thoracic tumor, whether aneurismal, cancerous, fibrous, fatty, steatomatous, or whatever it may occur, positively forbids assurance.

In passing from the consideration of the respiratory organs, it is not out of place to remark that, the whole thorax should be comprehended at a *coup d' œil*, and yet individual parts be thoroughly scanned. The unassisted ear, applied to the chest, will often gain a more satisfactory acquaintance with its general condition and vital capacity, than can be gained by the most expert use of the stethoscope. Whether the ear is applied directly to the chest, or a stethoscope is interposed, is not a matter of so much importance as that the examiner be able to hear with the ear, and correctly interpret the report of the organ.

IV.

Heart and Circulatory System.—The remark on page 21 may be repeated: "Organic disease of the heart positively excludes." Its acute affection or chronic lesion with marked rational symptoms will not, manifestly, be brought to the Insurance Examiner's attention; but as its lesions, even when giving rise to no inconvenience of which the party himself may be conscious, nevertheless are liable suddenly or slowly to cut short the life, it becomes absolutely essential to explore the slightest deviation from its normal condition.

LOCATION.—Recognized by its impulse, palpitation and percussion, the heart should occupy in relation to the thoracic wall a space about two inches in diameter vertically between the fourth and sixth ribs, and transversely a little to the left of the sternum—the impulse of the apex being about two inches below the nipple, and, varying with the size of the chest, an inch towards the mesial line.

Any change from this location requires inquiry as to its cause. Prominently among causes are to be mentioned; Pleuritic Effusions, whether of serum, pus, or air; Emphysema; Deposits in the Lung, whether tubercular, inflammatory, cancerous or other; Tumors; Dilatation of the Stomach, Enlargement of Liver, Ascites, &c.

BULGING OR DEPRESSION.—Protruding of the præcordial region indicative of Hydro-pericardium, or Hypertrophy of the organ. Depression, if considerable, indicative of previous Pericarditis with its contracted exudates and adhesions.

IMPULSE.—This is, as might be expected, normally stronger in persons of a lean habit than in the corpulent. Its location is changed by position, whether erect or supine; by distension of the stomach; by respiratory movements, &c. It is augmented in extent and intensity by hypertrophy. It is augmented in area of vibration, but diminished in intensity by dilatation or pericardial effusion, or fatty degeneration. A feeble impulse, irrespective of local lesion of the heart itself, may indicate cerebral disease, impoverished or morbid blood, or reflex influences of depression from disease of remote organs.

A broken or irregular impulse is suggestive of pericardial adhesions. When both a systolic and diastolic impulse are felt, hypertrophy with dilated ventricles is to be looked for. In connection with the impulse may be noticed the purring thrill of Laennec, suggesting possible presence of valvular stiffening. Vibration as of friction may be felt from roughened pericardial surfaces.

AREA OF DULLNESS.—The diameter indicating the approximation of the heart to the parietes of the chest may be extended by strong percussion, eliciting deep-seated dullness over the entire heart and large blood-vessels superior. But if without change in the strength of stroke, the area is materially increased, there is room for apprehension of fluid effusions in the pericardium or enlargement of the heart itself. Of course, local pleuritic effusion may be confounded with it, but to the examiner this is of little consequence, as either must reject, or, at best, postpone. The same remark may be made as to the differential diagnosis of Hydro-pericardium, and Concentric or Eccentric Enlargement of the Heart.

An apparent diminution of the area of dullness is noticeable during a deep respiration, but if very considerable, or there is abnormal resonance, there may be pulmonary emphysema, or hydrœria, either of which reject. In doubtful cases the applicant should be examined both in the erect and recumbent position. Abnormal dullness in the aortic region calls attention to the possibility of dilatation, or aneurism of the the great arterial trunk.

PULSATIONS.—In addition to the character of the impulse produced by the cardiac movements, it becomes necessary to note the *rhythm*, which may be varied in frequency, order of succession, and multiple character. Coincidently, with the pulse (p. 64 *et. seq.*) it may be increased or diminished in frequency, or it may become irregular or intermittent. Its normal range for insurance purposes is from sixty to eighty-five, or possibly ninety in the minute. Continuously above or below this standard should reject or postpone. But the great power of the nervous system over the contractions should be kept in mind. Mental excitement under the examination, in nervous subjects, will often throw the beats up to a hundred or more. If without this the applicant stands erect, and brings the muscles of the extremities into a state of contraction, voluntarily or involuntarily, the beats will readily pass the hundred. Hence the necessity of waiting examination until the effects of exercise or mental excitement have passed, and then, while the person is in the sitting or recumbent position, enjoining upon him as complete relaxation of all the muscles as possible. With due precautions, if there be not some fixed cause of a morbid character, apparent abnormalities in frequency may be made to disappear.

Extreme rapidity or palpitation (p. 28,) although generally accompanying some lesion of the heart, "bears no positive relation to any special cardiac malady, and is therefore not diagnostic of any." The symptom directs attention to possible cardiac lesion, but in the vast majority of instances to dyspepsia, impaired blood, or nervous disorder. Retardation of the pulsation points to some affection of the nervous centre, or degeneration of the cardiac parenchyma, or alteration of the aortic orifice. Irregularity of contraction is of rather more significance, as indicating valvular or parenchymatous local change, or grave lesion of the nervous centres or remote organs. Yet many cases occur where irregularity is the rule even during most perfect health. Hence, taken alone, it ought not to cause rejection. Palpitation with irregularity and deficient impulse suggests dilatation and weakened walls, although other physical signs may be wanting. In this case the rational symptoms, age, habits, condition of the digestive system, the blood, &c., will afford sufficient concurrent evidences to decide upon the real character of the case.

The intermittent pulsation may be an individual peculiarity in health, but generally indicates organic cardiac lesion, or some cause either temporarily or permanently impressing the nervous system. It is of graver character, on the whole, than either changes in frequency or regularity.

The relation of the systolic and diastolic sounds to the intervals of rest may be varied; more usually the longest interval is prolonged, which may depend on auriculo-ventricular stricture; or, again, the first sound may be prolonged over upon the second, suggesting "hypertrophy with stricture of the arterial orifices." In strongly marked cases of this kind the diastolic sound is sometimes wholly suppressed.

On the other hand, there may be heard three or four sounds instead of two, ascribable to important organic changes in the structure. The precise nature of these changes it is unnecessary to point out, as this abnormality must peremptorily exclude from assurance, whatever its plausible explanation.

CHARACTER OF SOUNDS.—The "dull, booming and prolonged" first sound of the heart, and the "short, abrupt and clear" second sound, in a condition of health are sufficiently distinct to be easily recognized, and when present for any even short period argue a healthy organ, but variation of these sounds may arise from incidental causes not implicating the structure. The healthy sounds when heard demonstrate—abnormal sounds throw doubt, and their cause must be cleared up.

Increased intensity of the sounds may depend on hypertrophy with dilatation, induration of the muscular tissue from carditis, or merely upon nervous excitability. They may derive increased loudness from solid or fluid deposits, in which case they are heard with distinctness at distant parts of the chest.

Feebleness of the sound may indicate fatty degeneration, or softening, atrophy, general debility, or accumulation of fluid in the pericardium; or, again, the interposition of the non-conducting emphysematous lung.

Increased *sharpness* may suggest thinness of the walls of the heart, as *dullness* points to hypertrophy and thickened valves.

A *dry* and *sharp* sound — increased tensity of the valves. *Hoarse* and *muffled*—a tumid condition of the same.

Metallic sound is usually dependent on gastric flatulency or nervous excitement, but sometimes due to stiffening of the muscular structure from old carditis.

The addition of a *bruit* to sounds is a circumstance which demands all the skill of the Examiner to appreciate in its bearings. The blowing sound may vary from the lightest murmur to the grating, rasping, and even whistling or musical sound. It is well to recollect that the intensity of the abnormal sound is not coincident with the extent of the lesion. The *bruit de soufflet* is caused by some obstruction to the free flow of blood through the heart and great vessels, or by a wrong composition of the blood, or nervous excitability. In the latter instances the *bruit* is often temporarily absent, but in case of organic lesion, the bellows-murmur, of greater or less intensity, *must always* be present.

The differential diagnosis of the immediate causes of the changed character of the sounds is not so important here, for when traced to actual organic lesion of the heart, the case must be rejected, whatever part of the structure is involved. But for convenience of reference Dr. Henry's diagnostic table is introduced:

BRUIT: If *systolic* and loudest at
  Base = AORTIC *obstruction*.
  Apex = MITRAL *insufficiency*.
BRUIT: If *diastolic* and loudest at
  Base = AORTIC *insufficiency*.
  Apex = MITRAL *obstruction*.
PULSE: If *regular*, full, or strong, jerking or resilient = AORTIC disease.
PULSE: If *irregular*, intermittent, unequal, soft, small, weak = MITRAL disease.

The systolic *bruit*, synchronous with the pulse and most audible at the apex, indicates mitral disease. The diastolic *bruit*, most audible over the centre of the sternum and along the course of the aorta, is indicative of aortic disease. Blowing sounds from functional disorder, impaired blood, etc., are usually soft — rarely harsh or musical. Although there is evidence that the *bruit* is occasionally an individual congenital peculiarity, nevertheless the rarity of such cases, and the difficulty of establishing their history, must preclude their acceptance. Recurrence to the historical and other rational symptoms, may convince that the abnormal sound does not depend on organic change, but while present it rejects or at least postpones.

LOCATION OF SOUNDS.— Effusions, tumors, morbid adhesions, etc., may displace the sounds laterally or antero-posteriorly. Descent of the sounds indicates hypertrophy with dilated auricles, or tumors at the base of the heart. Abdominal distension, by raising the diaphragm, may cause ascent of the sounds.

Friction sounds are indicative of changes in the serous lining of the pericardium, analogous to those which have been alluded to on the pleura, tending to adhesions, contraction and impairment of cardiac movements. When present they reject.

DISEASES.— Among those affections of the heart to which the examiner's attention is to be directed may be noted: Aneurism, Angina Pectoris, Adhesions, Atrophy, Cyanosis, Degeneration, Dilatation, Hypertrophy, Malformations, Myocarditis, Pericarditis, Valvular changes, and, lastly, disorders not involving apparent structural changes, but rendering its movements and sounds abnormal.

Aneurism may affect the wall of the heart, or the coronary arteries. Its symptoms and signs are alike obscure, but the possibility of a party, pronounced free from cardiac disease, dying suddenly from this lesion renders it desirable for the examiner to bear in mind its occasional occurrence—particularly when investigating obscure cases.

Angina Pectoris — that intense pain in the præcordial region, with suffocative sensations and fearful anticipations of sudden death — is generally indicative of fatty degeneration or obstruction of the coronary arteries. In all cases it rejects.

Adhesions, impairing the mobility of the organ, and most usually accompanied by lingering pericarditis, temporarily rejects. In such cases there is possibility of ultimate recovery.

Atrophy — diminished area of dullness, lessened intensity of sounds and impulse. This condition is invariably connected with such a degree of general cachexia, or debility, that the latter alone would preclude the risk.

Cyanosis, usually congenital, but not always — sometimes appearing late in life — is both incurable and subjects to the chances of sudden death.

Degeneration, ordinarily fatty and coincident with similar affection of the kidneys, liver, etc., rejects. It is tolerably recognizable by *exclusive* diagnosis. Feeble impulse, weak sounds, slownesss of pulse, occasionally dyspnœa with evidences of pulmonary congestion, general debility, giddiness, faintness, nervous exhaustion, etc. In all cases of obesity, especially where fattening has taken place rapidly, as often during convalescence from low fevers, the heart must be carefully inspected for signs of this grave change.

Dilatation may be coincident with hypertrophy, natural thickness of the wall, or with the latter attenuated. In the last mentioned form there are increased area of dullness, less powerful impulse, but increased intensity of sounds. The pulse is weak and irregular. Inactive capillary circulation in the extremities. Gastric and cerebro-nervous symptoms, dyspnœa, palpitation, etc. However mild the rational symptoms, the dilatation alone, if made out, rejects.

Hypertrophy, whether *concentric* or *eccentric*, declines the risk. It is usually connected with valvular obstruction, although hypertrophy of the right ventricle may depend on obstruction to the pulmonary circulation. Differential diagnosis is scarcely important here. Increased area of dullness, augmented impulse, less distinctness of systolic sound, and, usually, concurrent changes in the valvular sounds. Full and flushed face, headache, vertigo, cardiac uneasiness, pain or palpitation increased by exercise, dyspnœa, etc., may be acknowledged as present to a greater or less extent. The hypertrophy is rather the result of disease than a disease itself, but it is so fraught with danger that the applicant must be turned over to invalid companies.

Malformations and misplacements of the heart scarcely need more than an allusion in this place. Cyanosis, dyspnœa, palpitation and morbid sounds may be present. The malformed heart always vitiates the risk, even though signs of its injurious result be not discoverable. Congenital misplacement of the heart is so rare a phenomenon that, practically, it may be ignored. But if displaced by effusions, tumors, etc., the cause will be warrant for rejection.

Myocarditis is of importance to the examiner from its results, especially *softening* and *induration*. The latter may ultimate in a dense cartilaginous transformation of the tissue, or even osseous deposits. Evidences of either of these conditions utterly preclude acceptance of the applicant. (Vid. p. 21.)

Pericarditis often leaves behind it adhesions impairing the cardiac movements, or effusions impeding dilatation. The methods of diagnosis have been previously given. Entire absence of rational symptoms, and physical signs of lesion, must be insisted upon prior to insurance. Repeated attacks disqualify, whether any symptoms or signs of mischief are present or not.

Valvular changes, aside from their interference with the transit of blood through the heart, are significant of chronic Endocarditis, Bright's disease, Rheumatism, Gout, and various constitutional derangements of the system with impaired nutrition. So constant is this association that, when there is doubt as to the meaning of abnormal valvular sounds, judgement can usually be largely aided by careful attention to the rational evidences of these, to the superficial observer, apparently disconnected difficulties.

Aside from the cachexia determining valvular change, all forms are characterized by symptoms denoting interference with the capillary circulation. Hence the increased frequency of respiration, and the dyspnœa, or rather the peculiar breathlessness, under all those influences which tend to render the pulse more rapid. Even when there are few other noticeable symptoms, it will be found, on questioning, that the party sleeps at night with the head and shoulders unusually elevated. There will be evidence of *oppressed* respiration without actual dyspnœa, with semi-voluntary, deeper inspirations at short intervals. The movements are languid and the extremities, in the evening particularly, are apt to be puffy and swollen. A short, dry cough, palpitation, occasional headache, restless and disturbed sleep, and præcordial pains are often present, and usually attributed to dyspepsia by the patient. Hepatic venous changes and disturbed action of the kidneys are the almost natural sequences, and without due consideration there is a liability to refer all the unpleasant feelings of the individual to "functional" disturbances of these organs. In all doubtful cases, an investigation of the condition of the renal organs will throw much light on the diagnosis.

With the later symptoms and results of the valvular lesion the Insurance Examiner, as such, has nothing to do, but a few words with regard to the relative frequency of the varieties, and their comparative fatality, may not be considered out of place.

Aortic Obstruction is one of the most frequent results of chronic valvular disease, and is longer in producing fatal results. It involves slow dilatation of the left ventricle and thus renders the mitral valves insufficient, the consequence of which is mitral regurgitation, with symptoms of congestion of the lungs. In this obstruction there is, when the heart is beating forcibly, marked parietal vibration over the base of the heart and the aorta.

Aortic Regurgitation is also quite common, and affects similarly the ventricle and mitral valve. The pulse is peculiar—"short and jerking."

Mitral Obstruction is infrequent. It necessitates dilatation of the left auricle and pulmonary artery with engorgment of the lungs. The pulse is variable in force, but rapid. Cough, respiratory oppression, and general disorder follow, and death speedily ensues, usually from pulmonary œdema or apoplexy.

Mitral Regurgitation is the most easily recognized of all the valvular lesions. The mitral valve seems to be the favorite point of attack when rheumatism implicates the heart. The systolic murmur is manifested by the slightest changes, even when symptoms are absent. The blood, escaping the imperfectly closed orifice, is driven back upon the lungs, producing congestion, with feeble pulse and dusky complexion. The left side of the heart is dilated—the ventricle also being hypertrophied. There is a chest thrill, but it is not transmitted along the aortic trunk. The pulse is irregular and deficient in fulness and force.

Obstruction, and regurgitation, through the pulmonary orifices are so rare as, practically, scarcely to demand notice. Regurgitation through the tricuspid, however, may not infrequently occur as a consequence of dilatation of the right ventricle, which then becomes hypertrophied, the auricle and *vena cava* distended, and there is a strong tendency to congestion of the systemic and cerebral circulation.

So far as term policies are concerned, or invalid risks, simple aortic obstruction is by far the most favorable for assurance. Mitral and tricuspid regurgitations are the least so. A system otherwise in perfect order, may gradually adapt itself to the changed cardiac conditions, and life be prolonged indefinitely.

NON-ORGANIC DISEASES of the heart are capable alone of producing death, and hence, on determining the absence of organic lesion, they should not be dismissed unnoticed. Youths and young adults are liable to them to a marked extent. So also women about the climacteric period. They are the product of nervous exhaustion or oppression, of dyspepsia, gout and rheumatism. Sexual excesses, uterine irritation, over-use of narcotics and stimulants etc., readily beget them.

Palpitation and intermittent, irregular and feeble pulse may be associated with valvular murmurs, closely simulating those from organic disease. There may be præcordial pains, with occasional attacks of headache, giddiness, or even syncope. Violent pulsations of the larger arteries, and a *bruit* may be heard along their track. There may even be subcutaneous œdema.

Dyspnœa is rarely present, and at times the valvular sounds are healthy. All the symptoms are more strongly marked than in real organic disease. Careful analysis will detect differences not easily described. The concurrence of symptoms will develop a non-insurable condition, at least temporarily existent, in doubtful cases. Diagnosis from fatty degeneration will give the most difficulty. Frequent functional disorders increase the liability to ultimate organic diseases.

Generally the *blood murmurs* of non-organic affection are heard at the *base* of the heart, but occasionally, probably rarely, the murmur is to be heard over the centre of the heart, and becomes more distinct at the apex. In the latter case anæmia is usually so distinct as alone to decline the risk.

In the non-organic affection the signs of hypertrophy do not accompany the abnormal bruit. The murmur is heard along the blood vessels. It is followed by a short and sharp second sound. The murmur is almost invariably, notwithstanding the exaggeration of other symptoms, of a *soft* character.

But it must be confessed that it often requires the grestest tact to decide correctly in these cases. For the Insurance Examiner the best rule is to examine at different times and with the most rigid precautions against error, recollecting that when the "functional" disorder is so considerable as to give doubt of the presence of organic change, the party is uninsurable on that account alone.

DISEASES OF BLOODVESSELS.—The occasional occurrence of aneurism, without symptoms noticed by the patient, suggests attention. The aorta may be dilated, or so enlarged by aneurismal tumor, as to cause bulging of the thoracic parietes before its peculiar and ultimately terribly distressing effects are developed. Or it may cause what is supposed to be laryngitis, by pressure on the recurrent laryngeal nerve; or attacks of dyspnœa, analogous to paroxysmal asthma. When its graver influences are manifest, naturally, the sufferer will not present himself for assurance. But earlier examination may detect, along the course of the aorta, slight protusion and dullness over the surface. It is more resistant, and the systolic impulse is communicated strongly to the finger. There may be vibration, but this is not always present. The persistent systolic impulse at the point, together with the usually attendant dyspnœa, cough, frequent irregularity of the circulation, swollen veins of the neck, and thorax; sometimes diversity in the pulsations of the two radial arteries from pressure on the sub-clavian; contraction of a single pupil on the affected side, with more or less disturbance of remote organs, will enable a decisive judgment against the applicant. ' When evidences of intra-thoracic tumor are present, differential diagnosis is unnecessary, for any kind rejects, but it is well to bear in mind that aneurismal tumors constitute the largest majority.

The condition of tne arterial system, as a whole, here comes under review. Is there an aneurismal tendency, from disease affecting the arterial wall? Does the rigid inelastic artery of advanced age suggest the conditions of senile gangrene? Is the structure such as to endanger rupture and apoplectic extravasation in the brain? Do the veins show marks of tardy return of the blood? Has the valvular structure been obliterated and the varicose condition ensued? Extensive varicosities of the veins impair the risk, not solely from the dangers of rupture and hemorrhage, but because indicative of either a general tendency to disease of the venous system, or some obstruction which may be of permanent character on the proximal side of the enlarged vessel.

Extraordinary pulsatory movements of the arteries, as noticed particularly along the aorta, carotids and temporals, suggest anæmia, structural derangement of the digestive organs as in the gouty diathesis, or great excitability of the nervous system. In the female it is liable to be associated with uterine disease.

In some instances it is one of the concurrent evidences of abuse of alcoholic stimulants, tobacco, opium, etc.

V.

Abdominal Organs. — The historical indications may call attention to the condition of particular viscera, but in every case the general contour of the abdomen, its proportion, symmetry and movements should be observed. It is proportionately larger in children than in adults, and again with advancing age it becomes more protuberant. Obesity more speedily shows itself by large deposits on the omentum and in the abdominal walls. It may be distended by ascites, by accumulated gases or by tumors. It is more voluminous in females who have borne children. In the region of the epigastrium it is always enlarged after eating, but in many cases of dyspepsia it may become enormously distended by persistent flatulency.

The liver or spleen may be so increased in dimensions as to occupy, respectively, the greater part of the cavity. Mesenteric disease, ovarian growths, encysted fluid or solid tumors, accumulation of fæces and hernial protrusions, severally, may change its outline and indicate more or less grave results.

Retraction of the walls may call attention to general emaciation, exhausting chronic diarrhœa or dysentery, metallic poisoning, tuberculosis of the mesenteric glands, or occasionally fibroid or cancerous deposits at the orifices of the stomach. The shrunken abdomen warns of deficient nutrition and cachexia. It is also liable to be present in organic affections of the brain.

The contour and proportion are best observed in the erect position, but if circumstances require investigation of the exact condition of the viscera, the person should be placed in the recumbent position with the limbs flexed on the trunk. With proper precautions to relax the muscular investment, the outline and genera. condition of the contained organs can be ascertained with very great exactness, unless the party is very obese.

THE STOMACH, if abnormally distended, indicates impaired digestion, or an obstruction to the passage of the chyme from its cavity. Deficient secretion of the gastric juice, or deficient innervation with consequent loss of mobility, are suggested—the deficient innervation possibly dependent on cerebral lesion. Obstruction involves either temporary spasmodic action, or a thickened or carcinomatous pylorus, which latter may be detected by deep palpation.

The small or shrunken stomach accompanies weak digestive power and scanty nutrition.

THE LIVER enlarged, points to endemic influences and *portal venous congestion*, or such other causes as may produce the same result. Even dropsical accumulation may ensue, but as the cause is ordinarily temporary and removable, its previous occurrence does not decline, and its presence only postpones the risk. But enlargement from *hepatic venous congestion*, with or without dropsical effusion, prevents insurance, because dependent on thoracic obstruction to the circulation. Unless that obstruction is proved to have been only temporary, the objection is a fatal one. The diagnosis between these two forms is usually readily made out, and the important character of their diversity must fully impress the Examiner. The enlargement may be due to abnormal deposits in the parenchyma—to determine the character of these requires attention to the history, and establishment of the diathesis. If to be referred to abnormal deposits or growths, the case must be rejected.

Atrophy of the organ is generally connected with evidences of impaired digestion and secretion, which taken with the history, will suffice for diagnosis. In vastly the larger proportion of cases the small liver depends upon *cirrhosis*, and this produced by habitual use of alcoholic stimulants. In all cases this condition established, even without symptoms of its remote results, denies the risk. Its most obvious concurrent symptoms are disturbance of the stomach and obstinate diarrhœa. The superficial veins of the abdomen are apt to be enlarged; the skin is sallow, dry and rough. Dr. Budd asserts strongly: "Slight sallowness of complexion, a dull pain, or some degree of tenderness in the right hypochondrium, with occasional feverishness, in a person above the age of thirty, who has been long in the habit of drinking spirits to excess, are almost conclusive evidence of the existence of cirrhosis, even before there is any distinct proof that the circulation through the liver is impeded."

The same condition of the organ may be produced by various cachexiæ, particularly malarious and syphilitic poisoning, caries and necrosis. Whatever the cause, its presence rejects.

Degeneration of the parenchyma of the organ by fatty or amyloid deposits, begets a similar train of symptoms, but is generally associated with enlargement of its bulk. The diagnosis is facilitated by reference to the history of the case and concurrent symptoms. Both involve gastric derangement, tumidity of the spleen, diarrhœa and anæmia. The fatty degeneration may, however, be connected with more or less general corpulence, often gained rapidly, and in the latter case is always suspicious. From whatever cause arising, and however moderate the manifest symptoms, both varieties reject.

Acute Atrophy will not, from the activity of the symptoms, be presented to the Insurance Examiner.

Chronic Inflammation of the viscus, whether superficial or parenchymatous, is the not infrequent result of residence in tropical climates, or of intemperate habits, or cachexiæ. While present, it rejects, whether it has yet produced either hypertrophy, or atrophy, or any of the later symptoms of the disease. It is well to recollect that, under the influence of treatment, the person may suppose a cure to have been effected, and thus present himself for insurance. Nevertheless, the admitted occasional anorexia, diarrhœa, scanty urine loaded with lithates, sallowness, dryness and roughness of the skin, the *physiognomy* and progressive emaciation and debility, will sufficiently characterize the case.

Jaundice has been already referred to (p. 27). Since while present, in all cases, it at least postpones, its differential diagnosis is here scarcely necessary.

THE PANCREAS is rarely diagnosticated as the seat of disease. Its enlargement can usually be determined by palpation, and, from whatever cause, declines the risk. The increase of size is generally accompanied by tenderness, a sense of fulness or hardness, heat and constriction, anorexia, nausea and obstinate vomiting, or inodorous eructations, emaciation, debility, and mental depression.

THE SPLEEN is so frequently enlarged permanently, without any evidences of derangement of health, that unless the enlargement is excessive, forming abdominal tumor, or the signs of malarious or other cachexia are present, it may scarcely be considered as impairing the risk. Nevertheless, the frequent association of enlarged spleen, with degenerations of the liver and other organs, with affections of the lymphatic glands, with leukæmia, phthisis, etc., renders it incumbent upon the Examiner, whenever it is present, to make a minute and exhaustive survey of the organs individually and of the system as a whole.

THE INTESTINAL TUBE.—There may be physical evidences of distension of the intestines by tympanites, accumulated fæces, herniæ or tumors. But the attention of the Examiner is rather directed to the condition of the canal by historical or concurrent symptoms which indicate its condition. *Hernia* is noticed upon p. 31, *et seq.* Heterologous growths of any variety reject. Acute affections of the tube postpone. Chronic disorders and lesions may require careful investigation.

The most frequent cause of question is the presence of *chronic diarrhœa*, meaning by the phrase abnormal frequency and fluidity of the alvine evacuations. More important than these will be found the character of the discharge. There may exist a chronic catarrhal affection of the mucous membrane, wherein, with little or no noticeable disturbance of the health, the increased frequency and fluidity of the discharges is kept up by mere habit of the part, in accordance with a well understood physiological law. Or it may be a normal individual peculiarity. In such a case the risk may not be invalidated. But the fact that such a condition of the canal very generally denotes irregular habits of diet, the abuse of alcoholic stimulants or opium, or local disease of the adjuvant or remote organ, suggests caution. (p. 40.)

A very large proportion of those engaged in the recent war are subject to this form of diarrhœa, which, subsiding for a time, is readily provoked by exciting causes. In the absence of the evidences of ulcerations, organic affection of the liver or kidneys, scorbutus, tuberculosis or other cachexia, such cases need not necessarily be rejected, but very great care should be exercised. The evidences of deficient nutrition afforded by emaciation, or its correlative, fatty degeneration, disqualify. Thoracic obstruction to the circulation may ultimate in diarrhœa, and hence inquiry is directed to the heart, lungs, etc. Deficient frequency, or consistence of the evacuations, points to the mere habit of the parts, illustrating rather the distensibility of the large intestine than disease; or, it may remind of mechanical obstruction by bands of consolidated and contracted lymph from previous enteritis, or hernia, or the pressure of tumors, or hypertrophied viscera, or of defective secretions from the mucuous membrane, the liver, and pancras, etc.; or of the benumbing influence of retained excreta, or poisons received; or, deficient innervation from central disease of the nervous apparatus. The varying gravity of these causes renders their differential diagnosis a matter of great importance, in order that justice may be done both to the applicant and the company.

Among the lesions of the tube which give rise to the least marked symptoms, and yet pregnant of grave consequences, is to be noticed *Atrophy of the mucous membrane*—a condition frequently found in the tardily convalescent, and in those laboring under a more or less manifest cachexia, tuberculous, syphilitic, amyloid, etc. This may be present without apparent diarrhœa, costiveness or constipation. When present it is likely to invade the entire continuity of the membrane. Often all the symptoms observed are referred vaguely to dyspepsia, but it may have originated in a true cirrhosis from inflammation extending to the subjacent tissue. From whatever cause arising, it is among the reasons for rejection. The labial, buccal and pharyngeal membrane will exhibit the imperfect structure to the eye, whilst anæmia and debility are minatory, if not actually present—without seeming cause. There will be admitted anorexia, nausea on arising from the recumbent position; a sensation as though "food was never effectually swallowed, but stuck at the diaphragmatic entrance of the stomach, causing the peculiar feeling of weight which attends indigestion and the abundant generation of gaseous fluids."

Hæmorrhoids are occasionally of such severity and productive of such exhaustion, as alone to preclude insurance, but ordinarily they refer examination to their producing cause, which is usually some obstruction to the return of blood from the rectum. Thus habitual constipation, enlarged uterus, pelvic or abdominal tumors, a cirrhosed or congested liver, etc. Or they may indicate the general relaxation of the va.ve structure of the veins, resulting from residence in tropical climates, or diseases tending to produce congestion of the pelvic vessels.

Chronic Dysentery is noticed on page 40. "The prognosis is never very favorable"—but the diagnosis should be exact.

In a general survey of the alimentary canal and subsidiary organs, the relative power and perfection of the nutrient system should be comprehensively estimated. Upon it depends the entire superstructure of organization. Its condition modifies judgment as to the probable influence of both hereditary and acquired predispositions. It influences the prognosis as to the results of both acute and chronic disease. Even when organic diseases of grave character are unmistakably present, as developed by the expert diagnostician, its high degree of perfection is capable of masking and concealing the rational symptoms usually observable in less fortunate cases. Lesions, ordinarily confessed beyond the control of so-called medicines, sometimes disappear under the healing influence of healthy blood furnished to them by a powerful digestive apparatus. Thus vigorous digestion may aid the Examiner in conscientiously recommending a risk which has some notably objectionable features. Yet the same condition of the chylopoietic viscera, associated with organic changes, may add weight to the reasons for rejection. Witness the *bruit* of the heart's valves, while yet abdominal health is undisturbed. Witness the tuberculous deposit in the lung, which remains unheeded until some accidental cause impairs digestive energy, and then the softening, breaking down, and hectic speedily number the remaining days of existence. The judgment of the Examiner is the combined result of a multitude of perceptions, vivified by the educated reasoning faculty—as the body of man is made up from almost innumerable parts, controlled by the single principle of life.

THE KIDNEYS.—As in the instances previously cited, acute affections of the renal organs do not come within the scope of a life insurance examination, but their chronic lesions are so frequently obscure and so frequently misapprehended, both by applicants and physicians, and at the same time they are so dangerous in tendency that the Examiner should be "armed at all points" against mistakes in regard to them.

Enlargement of one or both kidneys from hypertrophy, cystic or heterologous growths, etc., may be discoverable as abdominal tumor. Whatever the differential diagnosis, such cases must be declined.

Chronic Inflammation is one of the forms of Bright's Disease to be presently discussed. It is noticed here as frequently confounded with simple nephralgia, spinal irritation, chronic rheumatism (lumbago), gout and scorbutic pains. The chronic nephritis absolutely rejects.

Nephralgia is often but the evidence of a temporarily, highly acrid and irritating secretion, or a "misplaced gout;" or the passage of what may prove but a single renal calculus; or it may be but an alternate of neuralgia, usually occurring in other parts, the effect possibly of malarious disease. It may be the temporary result of medicines or poisons, or, as in smallpox, perhaps from irritation of the specific virus. Or the real anguish may depend on enteritis. The diagnosis is to be *exclusive*—absence of the distinctive concurrent symptoms of the other affections noticed, must be determined. Nephralgia readily passes into nephritis, and unless the fact of its occurrence is an isolated one, and the phenomena definitely traced to a removable and removed cause, it should decline. Recurrent attacks are equally objectionable to the risk. (*vid.* p. 35 *et seq.*)

BRIGHT'S DISEASE, OR ALBUMINURIA.—Desquamative nephritis in the acute form, from its active symptoms, does not require notice here—but the chronic form may exist for a long time without marked symptoms, and hence a liability for both the applicant and the Examiner to overlook an uninsurable case of disease. Without actual sickness there may be general feelings of *malaise*, with imperfection of health and general debility. Anorexia or capricious appetite, with gastric and intestinal disorder, vomiting and diarrhœa, usually attributed to dyspepsia. Progressive emaciation, which, however, is sometimes concealed by the puffiness of anasarca, most noticeable on the face and eyelids, but gradually becoming general. The urine is passed more frequently than usual—the patient being obliged to rise in the night for the purpose. The urine may be normal in its appearance and chemical reaction, but microscopic examination will detect in the sediment disintegrated epithelial cells, or even fibrinous casts of *tubuli uriniferi* from the kidneys. The general aspect of the party will show the almost indescribable, but nevertheless characteristic physiognomy of renal disease. The skin is dry, rough, and sallow — in time becoming anæmic, waxy, and sodden. There are evidences of oppression in respiration from slight œdema of the lungs. Frequent local pains — most frequently cephalalgia, but invading any part, may be admitted, but are referred vaguely to dyspepsia, rheumatism, or neuralgia. These communicate a permanent expression to the facial lines. Disorders of vision are not infrequent, and the expert ophthalmoscopist can sometimes detect on the retina evidences that the supposed local affection depends upon organic lesion of the distant kidneys. Deafness and local paralyses elsewhere, may be the sole monitions of the renal affection. Supposed "functional," but ultimately clearly organic cardiac disease, may mask the real difficulty. In fine, a marked proclivity to local inflammation of whatever organ or surface, even though the party, at the time of the examination, be apparently in excellent health, lends color to suspicion of renal imperfection.

All the symptoms here recounted may be present in any of the forms of *Bright's Disease*, whether resolved into atrophy, cirrhosis, degeneration, or deposit. Save in so far as the accompanying cachexia of each may have its own bearing on the general character of the risk, their differential diagnosis is unnecssary.

Their ultimate result is the same—uræmic poisoning and death, which may be hastened by the concurrent affections of the heart, lungs, liver, general or local dropsy, etc.

The prognosis is always grave, and hence the subject uninsurable, even though temporarily there is an absence of symptoms. In all doubtful cases the urine should be tested in its specific gravity, its chemical reactions, and microscopy of its sediments. The peculiar fuliginous appearance sometimes present, probably from some chemical change in the hæmatin accompanying the desquamation, will readily attract notice. So also the presence of albumen, but particularly the low specific gravity, and the sediment composed of the epithelial casts and disintegrated blood cells. The tests are so simple, and so easily applied, that, while interests of such magnitude are in issue, there should be no excuse permitted for neglecting them. It should be borne in mind that *Temporary Albuminuria* may have been present, in connection with previous diseases, and yet complete recovery have taken place. Thus, in connection with Scarlatina and other exanthems, Cholera, Pneumonia, Rheumatism. Or again from confinement to an albuminous diet. Occasionally, also, during pregnancy. Probably in these cases there has been no considerable or continuous exfoliation of the epithelium of the *tubuli uriniferi*. Such cases may not, from their history, impair the risk. But it is unsafe to accept a case of *present* albuminuria, even though there may be strong belief that it is the simple form.

Calculus present rejects. Recurrent attacks also forbid the risk. But it may be recollected that popularly mere vesical pain and strangury are attributed to *gravel*, and hence, when this is spoken of, the case should be further tested.

Chronic Cystitis and *Enlarged Prostate* disqualify, and so, also, during its existence, *Permanent Stricture.* These lesions, on occurrence of slight exciting causes, may eventuate fatally. Spasmodic stricture is not infrequently symptomatic of renal lesion, and the chronic inflammation of the bladder may also be kept up by the deranged kidneys.

DIABETES may be noticed in this connection, although scarcely to be considered as a disease of the kidneys. From its insidious nature, and long absence of readily cognizable symptoms, it is liable to be overlooked both by the party applying and the too unobservant Examiner. Aside from the varying influences which, within the limits of health, may increase or diminish the amount of urine excreted, any undue quantity habitually passed should direct attention. Whether saccharine or not, the undue amount postpones. If repeated tests show the presence of sugar, or abnormal specific gravity, the risk must be declined. Absence of these, and increased amount, suggest Bright's Disease.

The skilled Examiner may often detect early the rational symptoms of the affection. The skin is dry, rough and shrunken, with a tendency to morbid nutrition of its appendages, or boils and carbuncles. Dryness, also, of the buccal membrane, with shrinkage of the gums. Unusual thirst and inordinate appetite, often resulting in distended stomach. Constipation, with dense and friable fæces. The odor of the breath sweetish, or, as has been suggested, chloroformic. Gradual emaciation, with muscular debility, and, occasionally, local paralyses. Slight, mental hebetude, with languid movements. Critical questioning may elicit the presence of diminished sexual desire and energy. In very many instances there may be superadded the signs of hepatic degeneration, and, always, disorder of the nervous system, manifesting itself in all phases, from mere dullness to irascibility, peevishness, capriciousness and monomania. By these nervous phases of the disease, the emaciation, and rough, dry integument, there is a *physiognomy* impressed upon the person which can scarcely escape the notice of the careful Examiner. In such cases the urine should be chemically tested by the most approved modern methods.

It is unnecessary to refer to the causation of diabetes, for its rational symptoms, when strongly marked, would cause rejection, whatever their cause, and the chemical evidences of its presence are totally exclusive.

ADDISON'S DISEASE, or that peculiar anæmic condition, with gradual bronzing in the color of the skin which, within several years past, has attracted the investigation of pathologists, need not here receive more than a passing notice. When it is possible to achieve an exact diagnosis, the concurrent symptoms will alone be sufficient to establish general disqualification.

VI.

Cerebro-Nervous System.—Very many of the notable disturbances of the orderly manifestations of the cerebro-nervous apparatus, are directly traceable to errors in action of the digestive organs. Hence consideration of the former, to be satisfactory in result, demands complete survey of the latter. Again, it often occurs that the apparent disorders of a part, or even the whole, of the nervous system, may depend upon reflex influences—local derangement of a single point begetting a train of symptoms which may be mistaken for those dependent on organic lesion of the nervous centres. Evidently, therefore, any judgment formed with reference to the symptoms only, is liable to be erroneous. Aberrations of nervous manifestations, if dependent on organic disease of the nervous centres, while present utterly disqualify—whatever their extent. But, if owing their origin solely to blood imperfectly formed, or rendered noxious by retained excreta, or poisonous material introduced into it, or, from reflex influences from lesions in other organs or tissues, the judgment, obviously, is to be shaped by considerations affecting the importance, extent, character, permanency or removability of the cause. This will thoroughly tax the skill of the Examiner.

It is well, in analysis of this branch of the subject, so far as it falls within the scope of the present essay, to adopt the simplest possible divisions. Thus we consider: Derangements of Motion, whether of the voluntary or involuntary muscles; Derangements of Sensation, whether common or special; Derangements of Mental Action, whether of the reason, or of the emotions.

DERANGEMENT OF MOTION.—Tremulousness, Tremors, Spasms, Convulsions, Error of Co-ordination, Rigidity, Paralyses, severally indicate a greater or less disorder of the nervous apparatus. It is necessary to inquire whether that disorder be dependent on local or general causes; whether it depend on nutrition, on toxæmia from retained excreta, or poisons taken into the blood from without, or upon organic changes at the nervous centre.

Tremor, or tremulousness, may be due merely to the changes of advanced age. If this sign of age comes prematurely, the premature age marks a condition of the system, as a whole, which lessens the desirability of the risk. Very frequently it is dependent on the use of tea, coffee, opiates or alcoholic stimulants; being the result of their action, although temporarily relieved by them. Concurrent symptoms here must be carefully scanned. The tremors of the opium eater, or spirit drinker, whilst deprived of the accustomed stimulus, should determine rejection. Metallic poisoning, as from lead, mercury, etc., may give the same result. Concurrent symptoms may determine morbid nutrition, or *exclusive* diagnosis may refer the feeble muscular agitation to central disease of the brain or spinal cord. But meanwhile it may be a nervous idiosyncrasy, or temporarily the result of reflex influences, from removable disease of remote organs.

Convulsions, or Spasms, sometimes readily occur in persons of a highly mobile nervous temperament. Hysterical females are especially liable to them, but males are not exempt. Like the milder symptom just noted, they may be of centric or eccentric origin. But ordinarily, when occurring without other evidences of cerebro-spinal lesion, they may be adjudged of eccentric origin. Among the causes of the latter variety, may be mentioned dental and intestinal irritation, more frequent in children, but not confined to them. Uterine, vesical and rectal irritation in the adult. Contaminated blood, from retained excreta or poisons, and powerful emotional influences. Among the centric causes, we advert to mal-nutrition of the brain, or its inflammation, deposits, morbid growths, sudden interference with the cerebral circulation, as by emboli, the shock of injury, hæmorrhage, effusions, etc.

Epilepsy, one of the forms of convulsive action, is distinguished prominently by its tendency to recur at intervals, which may be more or less distinctly periodic. The period between the paroxysms may show no marked derangement of health, although, unfortunately, there is likely to be mental hebetude and tardy development of all normal bodily action. Its peculiar suspension of consciousness serves to assist in diagnosing it from hysterical, and, indeed, most forms of convulsions. True epilepsy always excludes, whatever its supposed cause. Convulsions from other causes, must be measured by them, their permanence or removability, and by concurrent evidences regarding their centric or eccentric origin, and the respective bearings of these, rather than the accidental symptom. Generally speaking, recurrent convulsions, even from clearly mild and removable causes, should postpone until the tendency to them has entirely subsided. Local convulsive action of greater or less intensity and duration, accompanied with numbness and inability to move the part—or *cramp*, as popularly designated, is sufficiently common to persons in good health, and need not necessarily disqualify. But its occasional occurrence among the initiatory symptoms of central nervous lesions, or of metallic poisoning, or, as reflex from important remote organic disease, suggests inquiry into the real meaning.

Defective Co-ordination of the movements as exemplified in *Chorea*, but present in other cases without the intensity of contraction observable in that disease, points to a similar train of inquiries as to its causation. It is often one of the most insidious of diseases, occupying months or years in its full development. Thus in Duchenne's "*Progressive Locomotor Ataxia*," characterized by long antecedent impairment of vision, with inequality of the pupils, with wandering, brief but piercing pains, — "like electric flashes"—then vertigo and difficulty in maintaining the equilibrium, and in co-ordinating the movements, with local anæsthesia or paralyses. Functional concurrent disorders of the bladder and rectum. The necessity of a strong effort of the will, in connection with the usually impaired eyesight, impresses an unmistakable *physiognomy* on the case. Owing its causation, as it probably does, to atrophy or degeneration of the great nervous centres, and its prognosis always being grave, its incipient signs should be carefully explored.

Rigidity of the muscles is closely akin to paralysis. It may involve but few muscles, or as many as in half the body. It is so generally associated with organic disease of the brain, especially *ramollissement* that, unless traceable positively to some local cause, it must exclude.

Paralysis, if involving any considerable portion of the body, as *hemiplegia* or *paraplegia*, inexorably must meet with refusal. But many cases of local palsy, from definite local causes only, are not debarred insurance. Thus where a nerve has been divided by accident or surgical operation; the pressure of a removable tumor or growth; the presence of some foreign substance, as a bullet or splinter, etc.; or, wherever clearly referrible to the local lesion alone. Again, paralysis, as well as convulsions, may be reflex, and the lesion at the excitor point be capable of relief. Local vicissitudes may beget a local paralysis of motion, as when, *e. g.*, the facial muscles of one side are temporarily paralyzed by exposure to a draft of air. In like manner the muscles of articulation may, by paralysis, beget aphonia. Pressure on a nerve from mere position, local shock from a blow, or common inflammation may ensue in palsy of the parts to which that nerve is distributed. Such cases need not necessarily be rejected, but the large proportion of cases, wherein this symptom is a concurrent one of diseases of the brain or spinal cord, requires the most minute and exhaustive research. Occasionally it may happen that the loss of mobile power will be found dependent on the influence of some pervading poison, *e. g.* lead, toxæmia, etc.

DERANGED SENSATION may be observed as affecting nerves of common or special sense. Of the former, *pain* is the prominent exponent; but sensations of heat or cold, itching, tingling, formication, pressure, etc., may co-exist, or be the sole manifestation. *Mutatis mutandis*, the same considerations enter into examination of the case, as in instances of deranged motion. There is, however, this important diversity, that the intensity of deranged sensation has no such constant relation to the severity of the cause as exists in disordered movements. The commingling of mental emotions may magnify or diminish the real importance of the symptom. It is well remarked: "That acute sensibility is not of necessity inflammatory, is one of the triumphs of modern pathology."

Diminished sensation is more analogous in its indications to paralysis of motion, than is hyperæsthesia to tremor or convulsion. It is more liable to be connected with central organic disease, or some overpowering general poison. Extended anæsthesia, over a considerable surface, is exceedingly apt to be connected with central ganglionic nervous lesion. But sometimes even the small and circumscribed part, which has become thus affected, is among the premonitory evidences of brain or spinal disease. In such cases the method of exclusive diagnosis will clear up the difficulty. It may depend on local influences, upon poisons in the blood, or other abnormal conditions of that fluid, (*e. g.* rheumatism), or be the characteristic symptom of certain cutaneous eruptions.

The *Special Senses* may present a similar variety of perversions from merely local causes, reflex influences, impaired or poisoned blood, or central disease of the brain.

DERANGED INTELLECTION acknowledges the same variety of causation, and while present positively declines the risk, whichever may have been the immediate source of disturbance.

DISEASES.— Among the forms of disease of the brain, against which the Insurance Examiner must put himself on guard, as liable to be masked by general indications of fair health, are to be noted: Chronic Meningitis, Apoplexy, Deposits or Growths, Ramollissement, Insanity, Atrophy, and, not the least in frequency, Chronic Poisoning. As affections of the Spinal Cord: Chronic Inflammation, Softening, Degeneration, or other evidences of its deranged nutrition.

ENCEPHALITIS of the acute form possesses sufficiently distinctive symptoms. But it may, from the beginning, be sub-acute, and readily lapses into the chronic character. In the latter case, the brain substance is likely to become implicated, with more or less modification of phenomena presented. There may be very slight vascular or general disturbance, but careful investigation may detect more or less distinct evidences of lesion. If the pulse is perceptibly affected, it is likely to be slower, or irregular and intermittent. A little impairment of the special senses; it may be hesitation or stammering in articulation, which afterward, perhaps, will deepen into complete aphasia, constant, deep-seated headache, nausea and vomiting, general *malaise;* some stiffening of particular muscles; limited paralysis, either of motion or sensation, or both; sluggish action of the secretory organs, with constipation and unusual retention of urine. Some peculiarity of mental manifestation, "eccentricity," hypochondria, or preternatural elevation of spirits, or unusual proclivity to entertain false or absurd notions. Restless vigilance may alternate with profound sleep, with, ordinarily, stertorous respiration. The occurrence of previous traumatic injury of the head, or of some disease tending to affect the brain, will throw light on the diagnosis. Location of the cause of these symptoms in the brain, will frequently require the *exclusive* method of diagnosis.

APOPLEXY.— Undoubted apoplexy previously occurring, although the party be now in apparently perfect health, peremptorily rejects. The Life Insurance Examiner is called upon rather to study premonitions — the forerunners of the lesion before it makes its appearance. The apoplectic habit is popularly supposed to be one where there is corpulency with a short neck, a florid face, and injected conjunctiva; the latter appearances more marked in cases of excitement, and accompanied with a sensation of fullness of the head, or vertigo and throbbing of the carotid and temporal arteries. If apoplexy occurs in individuals of this *physique,* it is rather because of fatty degeneration of the organs, than the condition of rude health supposed present. Or, as in very many cases reported, there was uræmia or other toxæmic causes of congestion of the brain, mistaken for real apoplexy. The tendency to the so-called congestive or serous apoplexies, is to be elucidated by studying the mal-action of the nutrient, secretory and excretory organs.

True apoplexy involves hæmorrhage into the tissue or cavities of the encephalon, and this presupposes degeneration of the tissue involving the coats of the supplying arteries, or, the originating lesion may be confined to the arterial wall. The symptoms of real apoplexy are closely simulated by the detachment of embolon, and its projection into, and consequent closure of, some important artery of supply. The existence of aneurism, save from simply traumatic causes, always should suggest examination, so far as possible, of all the arterial trunks. Whatever interferes with the activity of the circulation, when the arterial parietes are weakened by calcareous or other abnormal deposits, by fatty degeneration or arteritis, etc., may at once involve apoplectic seizure in the midst of apparent high health. Thus muscular efforts, mental influences, especially of the emotional kind, disordered digestion, stimulants or narcotics, febrile accessions, retained excreta, etc. Not only persons of "full habit," but those of spare frame, long necks and scant blood, may die of it from similar exciting causes. There may be none of the commonly supposed *prodromata* present, and yet the party be on the verge of an attack. Something more than head symptoms are to be looked for. When "shadows are cast before," they are manifested " by great depression of spirits, by attacks of loss of memory, by illusions, by vitiated perceptions, by vertigo, by odd sensations in the head;" but these are rather the indications of the degeneration than of the coming apoplectic seizure.

DEPOSITS or GROWTHS of an abnormal character will vary in the symptoms presented, according to the part of the encephalon invaded, and the degree of mischief or size of growth. The symptoms are often obscure, and their character opined from the diathesis or cachexia present. *Exclusive* diagnosis is the most satisfactory; the most common symptoms being " headache, sickness, mental depression with confusion, partial paralysis, and epileptiform convulsions."

ATROPHY of the encephalon is usually the condition of senility; but it may occur in the child or adult, as the result of those lesions which cut off the supply of blood—*e. g.* pressure of tumors or growths, embolon, ligature of arteries, etc. Advancing insidiously, it may ultimate in utter dementia.

HYPERTROPHY is very rare, but sometimes is noticed in adults between twenty and thirty. It seems more probable that what is denominated hypertrophy of the brain, is rather a disease of its bony case, involving replacement of the cartilaginous substance, by abnormal calcareous deposit. Hence, the unchanging cranial wall develops the effects of gradual and prolonged pressure upon the contents. This increased density and hardness of the bone is gained at the expense of its elasticity, and hence, in such cases, there is unusual fragility of the bones everywhere. Repeated fractures of bones from slight causes, with any of the ordinary evidences of cerebral disorder, direct attention to the condition described. It is fatal to the risk.

SOFTENING (*Ramollissement*) of the encephalon is one of the most covert and insidious and, at the same time, one of the most frequent and dangerous lesions of the brain which the Examiner is called upon to discover. Noticeable enough in the acute form, it may advance from utter obscurity with steps so treacherous and and stealthy, that only the wariest observer can gain a clue to its presence, or avoid sometimes confounding it with trivial affections. Softening may occur as one of the results of acute inflammation, or, as a consequence of senility. But without any such history it may come on gradually, at any age, as the result of those causes which beget local or general degeneration. Thus mal-nutrition, diseased arteries, emboli, typhoid or other deposits, fatty degeneration, etc. The functional disorder of the brain, taken with the concurrent symptoms, will clear up the diagnosis. The evidences of chronic (white) softening are similar to those of the acute inflammatory (red) form, differing mainly in their intensity and duration. The great difficulty is in assigning due weight to those diseases of other organs, to which the brain symptoms may be only secondary, and here, again, the *exclusive* method of diagnosis becomes indispensable. Unless clearly attributable to remote lesions of a removable character, a case which has presented suspicious brain symptoms should be declined. Among these suspicious symptoms, we note paroxysmal headache, aggravated by noise, light, exercise, etc.; nausea and vomiting with, — — generally, constipation, which are not traceable to deranged digestion; lessened sensibility of the bladder; vertigo, nervousness, hypochondria, diminution of mental powers, with obtuseness of special sensation. Sensations of "prickings and twitchings in the limbs, sometimes pain, and sometimes numbness." Local cramps, and more or less permanent rigidity of particular muscles. General feebleness of the muscular system, and hebetude of all the faculties. A feeble, irregular and intermittent pulse. The party may confess difficulty in "collecting his ideas"—there is a little hesitancy of speech, a little delay in answering questions—a little appearance of abstraction, and the articulation not quite perfect.

If historically there has been some disease or cachexia present, which notably affects the encephalon—some local injury from a fall, or blow, or surgical operation, and especially if the age is above fifty—the diagnosis is strengthened, that softening, or some equally important lesion of the brain, is present. The *physiognomy* of the affection is very impressive; in fact, scarcely to be mistaken.

In passing it may be remarked, that a condition very analogous to chronic softening, with its attendant symptoms, is very frequently observable after severe COUP DE SOLEIL. In cases of the latter the prognosis is not as grave, nevertheless, as it is capable of passing into actual ramollissement, with paralysis, insanity, etc., wherever the party has been so affected, the examination should be cautious in the extreme.

CHRONIC POISONING of the brain may occur from the habitual use of Alcoholic Stimulants, Opium, Tobacco, "Hasheesh," even Tea and Coffee, and, indeed, a great variety of agents taken for the purpose of exhilaration or soothing. During the use of the narcotic, the individual may, so far as external indications are concerned, be on the level of perfect health; but, let any accidental physical cause interfere with its usual impression, or let its use be suspended, and the condition of *Nervous Asthenia* immediately supervenes. A similar condition is often observable in those whese mental faculties have been overwrought, and it engenders an almost uncontrollable desire for stimulants or anodynes—which latter then get the discredit of its production.

"Physicians," says Dr. Flint, "are often consulted by patients who, although far from being well, have no well-defined malady. They complain of languor, lassitude, want of buoyancy, aching of the limbs, and mental depression. They are wakeful during the night, and enter upon their daily pursuits with a sense of fatigue. Under the pressure of mental excitement, they may be able to exert themselves, but, when the excitement subsides, they are jaded and worn out. They become apprehensive that their powers are giving way, and are apt to fancy the existence of some serious malady. An investigation of the different organs of the body reveals no evidence of disease; the lungs, heart, kidneys, etc., are sound. None of the affections embraced in the nosological catalogue may be discovered, yet the morbid condition is real."

A person in this condition is, clearly, laboring under the result of undue changes in the minute structure of the brain, precisely analogous to those which occur from chronic poisoning. The expert Examiner will recognize the symptoms when present, or, if temporarily held in abeyance by the accustomed excitation, will scan closely the history, as given by the applicant and sustained by the friend and physician. Although the prognosis, under correct therapeutic and hygienic treatment, may be pronounced by the physician not grave, the uncertainty of this being carried out, and its dangerous tendency if neglected, precludes, utterly, acceptance of the risk.

Delirium Tremens, Dipsomania, etc., previously existent, imperil the risk. It is only after the lapse of a long period of time and great weight of collateral moral evidences of reform, that a party who has suffered from them can be accepted.

INSANITY.—Some general observations on this subject have been made on page 25, *et seq*. In this place, we refer rather to the detection of incipient or of masked insanity. The importance of this topic demands that it shall receive the most careful attention of the Examiner. Distinct cases, or those connected with obvious disease of the nervous centre, of course will not be presented for insurance. But the cunning maniac, with proverbial ingenuity, has been known to outwit examiners, and secure large policies upon his dangerous life. Hence, clear ideas upon its diagnosis become as indispensable to the Insurance Examiner as to the Medical Jurist.

The Family History first calls attention to the point, as it is well recognized as one of the most commonly transmissible of affections. It is safe to say that in from one-third to one-half of all cases of obvious insanity, its presence in the family within three generations can be traced. If those slight aberrations of mind or eccentricities, which, from absence of existing causes, do not deepen into such mania as requires treatment, were taken into account, the proportion would certainly be largely increased.

Atavism is here frequently witnessed. Baillarger's propositions appear to be generally confirmed:

"The insanity of the mother, as regards transmission, is more serious than that of the father; not only because the mother's disorder is more frequently hereditary, but also because she transmits it to a greater number of children.

"The transmission of the mother's insanity is more to be feared with respect to the girls than the boys; that of the father, on the other hand, is more dangerous as regards the boys than the girls.

"The transmission of the mother's insanity is scarcely more to be feared, as regards the boys, than that of the father; the mother's insanity, on the contrary, is twice as dangerous to the daughters."

To these it may be added that the insanity of brothers and sisters respectively, is a matter of even more import, as establishing the family proclivity, than that of parents.

The hereditary tendency follows the same law as other inherited tendencies, as to its occurrence at certain ages. (*Vid. pp.* 8 and 47.)

A similar rule obtains as to resemblances between parents and particular children. (p. 46.) Owing to the absence of exciting causes, the hereditary predisposition may never have been manifested in any striking derangement, and yet the observant Examiner may notice in the temperament, in the habits of life, in the occupation, the peculiar features of intercurrent diseases, domestic or civil troubles, etc., additional reasons for declining the risk. Pursuits which subject to great mental "wear and tear," and intemperance, are among the most potent of predisposing influences. Many cases are vaguely attributed to religious excitement, grief, joy, fear or other emotions, but it is safe to assume that when insanity ensues upon them, it is because the nervous centre is already on the brink of disease.

There are unusual difficulties attendant upon the decision in suspicious cases. But the Examiner at least escapes the necessity of determining the difference between *feigned* and real insanity. The trouble will be in baffling the great ingenuity with which the party will often conceal the mental disorder. As Bucknill and Tuke remark:

"The dread of insanity in many families of this kind is so great as to constitute, in itself, a morbid feeling sufficiently strong to mislead the observation, to warp the judgment, and to occasion sins of concealment and untruthfulness towards those who have a right to expect, and to demand the fullest and most explicit confidence."

Next to the hereditary predisposition, may be mentioned that arising from the temperament, either original or acquired. Although examples of insanity may be found in any described temperament, yet in the

Sanguine or Phlegmatic they are about invariab.y connected vith notable organic lesion. In the pure Nervous temperament, or particularly in the Bilio-Nervous or Melancholic variety, it is apt to occur with very little or no evidence of internal lesion aside from the mental disorder. The form of insanity which occurs to the melancholiac is that which is most likely to come before the Examiner. There is usually deficient energy of digestion, with costiveness and constipation; pale and abundant, or scanty urine loaded with lithates; pulse, soft and compressible; skin, sallow, hard and dry, or sometimes cool and clammy. "The complexion of the insane person is never clear and healthy." Fixed dull pain may be complained of in the head, or, at least, a sense of oppression. There are impassive, immobile features, with a moody or saddened expression. "The eyes are motionless, or directed towards the earth or some distant point; and the look is askance, uneasy and suspicious." In the more distinctly nervous temperament there is, as would be expected, a more changeful countenance, and a greater activity of movement. There is loquacity, and varied emotions lend vivacity to the features; the eye is quick and flashing; the skin dry, and more florid in parts, with unnatural pallor in others; the pulse is rapid, but feeble and jerking. There are derangements of the secretions, irregular and capricious appetite, and tendency to emaciation. Indeed, defective nutrition is so large an element in the etiology of insanity, that some high authorities attribute to it the whole disease. All diseases which notably impair the constitution of the blood may awaken, or exaggerate, the hereditary or acquired predisposition. Unfortunately the converse is not always true: insanity once existent, with evident poor bodily health, is not always removed when health seems thoroughly restored. The worst cases, notoriously, are those which manifest mental derangement with high health. Briefly: In making up an opinion in a suspected case, in addition to the family history, the habits of eating, drinking, sleeping, and occupation; the diseases previously existent; the exact present condition of the digestive and cerebral organs; the peculiarities in surroundings, dress, bearing, and expression, as contrasted with the antecedent usage; and, finally, the general physiognomy of the case are each to be fully investigated. In the absence of glaring evidences of eccentricities, or peculiarities, as compared with those which sane people may exhibit, the individual must be compared, or contrasted with his previous self, and then the change, if any, be traced to its real cause.

SPINAL DISEASES.—*Spinal Inflammation* of the chronic form, whether of the meninges or substance, is an insuperable obstacle to insurance. The comparatively light local symptoms frequently cause it to be confounded with rheumatism or neuralgia, but careful examination will ordinarily elicit the presence of a much greater general disorder than would occur in such cases.

There is generally a fixed pain, usually high up on the vertebra, slight tenderness on percussion or deep pressure; the pain aggravated by movement, especially if quick. The passage of a hot sponge over the part is also likely to give increased pain. There is a liability to spasms or paralysis, particularly of the muscles of the neck and back, upon the occurrence of exciting causes.

The occurrence of curvature with these evidences of local lesion, adds to the certainty of diagnosis.

Spinal Irritation, or that ill-defined assemblage of hyperæsthesia, nervous excitability, with disturbances of remote organs, whatever its real pathology, is usually accompanied by such evidences of digestive, thoracic, or cerebral disorder, that they alone suffice for rejection without differential diagnosis.

PARALYSIS, of whatever degree, whether dependent on Morbid Nutrition, Degeneration, Tumors, Apoplexy, Traumatic Lesion, or Softening, always disqualifies.

The trouble in diagnosis here, is mainly due to the imagination of the patient. Without actual paralysis, either of motion or sensation, there is often Deficient Innervation. There is a sense of weakness of the knees, with slight numbness or prickling sensation; a loss of perfection of the muscular sense; disturbance of the function of the organs of the trunk on the level of the lesion—thus disturbed respiration and circulation, disturbed digestion, slow and imperfect extrusion of the fæces and urine. The genital system is depressed in activity; the muscular tissue wastes, and nutrition generally is imperfect. The brain sympathizes more or less, and spasmodic contraction may alternate with the paralysis or deficient power of motion.

The history of the case will here throw light upon the symptoms present. A blow, a wrench, a concussion; exposure to cold and moisture; excessive fatigue, long continued cramped positions incident to various occupations, certain morbid habits and indulgences, mineral poisons, hereditary predispositions, and cachexia, severally, may be identified as originating the difficulty. On the other hand, hypochondria and hysteria may imitate the symptoms very closely. There is a large amount of vulgar literature afloat which serves to torture young adults, especially, with the idea that the dreaded *tabes dorsalis* has already seized upon them. Half of the symptoms in these cases depend upon dyspepsia, and two-thirds of the balance upon the imagination of the victims.

VII.

Miscellaneous Affections.—*Psoas and lumbar abscesses* while present reject; and even when recovery seems perfect, from their great tendency to return, throw doubt on the propriety of accepting the applicant. All *abscesses* of any considerable extent postpone. Recurrent abscesses involve suspicion of some cachexia. Even *furunculi* should not lightly be passed over, and *carbuncles* reject.

Open *ulcers* and obstinate *cutaneous affections* are so generally connected with constitutional taint, or permanent lesion of nutrition, that the case is rendered doubtful by their presence.

Large or extensive *varicose veins*, *chronic* and numerous *enlargements* or *induration of the lymphatic glands*, *fistulæ* (p. 22, *et seq.*), *morbus coxarius*, or acute or chronic inflammation within, or about any of the larger joints.

Irreducible hernia, double hernia.

Excessive loss of structure, as amputations above the middle third of the thigh, or at the shoulder joint.

Tumors of a non-malignant character, but involving danger by their anatomical position, or as requiring a severe surgical operation.

All tumors or growths of a malignant or scrofulous nature; Exostoses, Enchondroma, etc.

Loss of sight or hearing from accident or causes not involving disease of the cerebral centres, nevertheless impair the risk, as subjecting the unfortunate subject unduly to injuries which the deprivation of the special sense does not permit him to avoid.

Finally, diseases which may have been present, but from which there seems to have been perfect recovery, not infrequently leave discoverable effects and influences to the educated eye, which materially lessen the life expectation.

VIII.

Female Applicants. — Although some companies decline all female risks, it is safe to say that, taken together, they are equally eligible as those of males. As before remarked, even the child-bearing period does not bring to them a mortality, materially preponderant over that of males of similar age. Indeed, if anything, the exposures and vicissitudes to which males are ordinarily subjected, during the active years of adult life, more than balance, in fatal results, the incidents of the female life during this period.

Certain anatomical differences with regard to the height, weight, chest measurement, and capacity, have previously been noted. (p. 54.)

There is, numerically, a greater proportion of nervous temperaments, and the modes of life more frequently expose to the evils of deficient ventilation and sedentary habits. But to these their systems become accustomed, by well known physiological law, so that not as deleterious results are produced as would be in the male.

The regularity and perfection of the menstrual function is to be ascertained; it being remembered that individual peculiarities in this respect are to be weighed rather in their relation to the general health than with reference to exact rules. If there is good health otherwise, irregularities in the menstrual function scarcely impair the risk. But at the climacteric period, the difficulties incident to the cessation of the function must be carefully inquired after. This is an objectionable time to insure; but in the absence of notable disturbance of the general health, or evidences of local disease, the party need not be declined. An anæmic or chlorotic condition, or signs of the cancerous cachexia will exclude.

Primary gestation impairs the risk, but, if this proceed without difficulty or danger to its termination, subsequent pregnancy need not be considered as adding to the risk. Statistics are said to show that the mortality from first labors, and ensuing puerperal fever, is about twice that of all ensuing labors up to the ninth; after the ninth, the danger is increased with each succeeding pregnancy and parturition. Whether this proportion is closely approximated or not, there is no doubt of the general truth of the proposition.

Labors requiring instrumental assistance, miscarriages, or repeated mal-presentations, or hæmorrhage, impair or exclude the risk. The occurrence of Puerperal Fever, or Mania, also declines. Remarkable varicosity of the veins, *phlegmasia dolens*, dropsical effusions, etc., are equally objectionable. Vesico-vaginal, or rectal fistulæ, or lacerations, also, while present, exclude. Emaciation and exhaustion, during lactation, also militate against assurance. Chronic Metritis or Sub-involution, deep ulcerations and profuse leucorrhœal or purulent discharges, at least, postpone.

But it should be recollected that mere dyspeptic derangements, or the *habit* of the parts, may keep up apparent symptoms when important organic disease has passed away. The real condition of the general health is here the point to be investigated.

It is unnecessary to remark, to the experienced practitioner, that organic uterine disease is vastly less frequent and important than is claimed by the specialists. The symptoms paraded as proving its existence, in the large majority of instances, being due to totally different causes. Even if it would be permitted, it is doubtful whether, so far as insurance is concerned, specular or digital examination would give any valuable information aside from that which can be gathered from the history and the general symptoms presented. Cases which suggest such examination to the family physician, so frequently have concurrent evidences of disease, that differential diagnosis becomes unnecessary, for these alone decline.

The facts with regard to the transmissibility of hereditary diseases, insanity, etc., in certain instances, rather to the females than to the males of the family, and *vice versa*, may have weight in deciding upon the risk. (p. 126.)

IX.

General Character of the Risk.—The systematic survey which has been taken of the history of the applicant, and the present condition of the individua' organs and functions of the body, is merely preparatory to answering the all important question propounded by the Insurance Company: "Do you RECOMMEND THE RISK?" This question should be answered definitely and distinctly—YES, or No.

But, before answering it, there are certain general considerations which it is necessary to have fully in mind. These are derived from the *general physiognomy* of the case as indicating the CONSTITUTION. Unde this somewhat indefinite designation we refer to the Temperament, the Diathesis, or the Cachexia of the party.

The *Temperament* has already been referred to, (p. 61 *et seq.*) Here the question arises: Is the party so situated that his peculiar temperament modifies the character of the risk? And in answering this, the same principles of prognosis are involved as in weighing its relation to present acute disease.

The *Diathesis* bears the same relation to disease that the temperament does to health. Original or acquired abnormalities in the organs determine, on the occurrence of any special disease, a modification in its course or tendencies, which assimilates its changes and symptoms to those which are especially peculiar to the diathetic infirmity. In the absence of exciting cause the diathesis may be apparently latent. In the absence of direct manifestation it may sometimes be cogently inferred from the family or personal history, or from the obvious results of previous disease. Each impresses its own physiognomy. Among those diatheses prominently demanding study, may be mentioned the *Strumous*, ultimating in scrofulosis, or tuberculosis, and characterized by defective nutrition, imperfect assimilation with consequent impaired function of the organs, with slow and deficient reparative power.

The *Gouty* or *Rheumatic* diathesis, characterized by "a predisposition to the undue formation of uric acid, and to congestion, irritation or inflammation of the muscular and sero-fibrous tissues, of the vascular system, of the serous membranes, and of the peritoneum." The development of, on the one hand, gouty affections, and on the other, rheumatic disorders, seems to be due to the relative conditions of the skin, and digestive mucous membrane.

The *Adipose* diathesis is marked by its results. Ordinarily there is deficient digestive energy and muscular weakness The viscera are large, but notably inactive

The *Phlogistic*, usually engrafted upon the Sanguine Temperament, where acute inflammation, with active symptoms, readily supervenes upon slight causes. Here there is generally great activity of the blood making processes, with some imperfection of structure of the excreting organs.

The *Typhoid*, when with rapidity of textural changes, easily exaggerated by disturbing influences, there is feebleness of nutrition and repair with inactivity of the excretories.

In fine, the acute physician may recognize a great number of these general proclivities to disease, yet each consistent with present health, which, being known, must enter into his well compacted decision as to the real character of the risk.

The *Cachexia*, unlike the Temperament or Diathesis, determines the presence of disease,—not, perhaps, involving any particular organ, but pervading, in its malign influence, each and all. It may be the diathesis developed into an existent disease. The diathesis, being known, may never find development into cachexia or local disease, being prevented by appropriate hygienic influences. But the cachexia may originate without the previous existence of the diathesis, and, in this case, is usually more amenable to therapeutics. When both co-exist, the prognosis is thereby rendered vastly more grave than it would be even with greater severity of local symptoms.

The noticeable cachexiæ are those connected with the developed diathesis, as above suggested, and to these may be added, as requiring attention, the Syphilitic,

Erysipelatous, Anæmic or Chlorotic, Albuminoid, Hæmic, Hæmorrhagic, Rachitic, Cancerous, etc.

The sum total, so to speak, of the power of carrying on the processes of life, ministering to repair, and resisting morbific influences, derived by the system as a whole, is expressed by the term the CONSTITUTION. This word is significant of the Vital Force, or individual capacity for living. It measures, for the Examiner, the Life-Expectation. Deviations from the typical standard of formation and action, as arbitrarily established for purposes of scientific comparison, may be found present to an indefinite extent, and yet the capacity for living be fully equal to, or even above the Insurance Average.

Poetical descriptions, or ideas, of the *mens sana in corpore sano*, may differ as widely as men themselves, and it is idle to set up either Apollo or Vulcan as types of Methuselah. Nay, the educated intellect, by adapting the frail body appropriately to its surroundings, may cause its years to surpass those of the most symmetrical and well developed athlete.

APPENDIX.

Note to page 15. (Occupation.)

Occupation has, of course, a more or less direct bearing on health and longevity: in some vocations there is constant danger of accident or violent death even, while in others the danger on this account is so slight as to be quite unworthy of consideration at all. Again, a particular calling may involve not the least risk on account of physical danger, and yet be extremely prejudicial to health and longevity. The following table indicates approximately the relative influence of the various callings and professions on the duration of life; Class I being considered most dangerous, Class IV least so:

CLASS I.

Brakeman on Freight Trains.
Buzz Sawyer.
Circular Sawyer.
Powder Maker.
Seaman.

CLASS II.

Bridge Builder.
Boatman.
Barber on Steamboat.
Brakeman on Mail Trains.
Cartridge Maker.
Clerk on River Steamboat.
Captain of Lake or Sea Vessel.
Car Coupler.
Conductor on Freight Trains.
Cooper.
Dock Laborer.
Engineer on River Steamer.
Farrier.
Fireworks, Maker of.
Fireman (Locomotive).
Grinder of Edged Tools.
Horse Shoer.
Laborer, (Wharf, Warehouse, Grain Elevator.)
Lighterman.
Lumberman.
Master or Mate of Vessel.
Match Maker.
Mail Agent, (Travelling).
Mate of River Steamer.
Miner (underground).
Nightman.
Pilot.
Quarrier.
Quarryman.
Raftsman.
Railroad Engineer.
Race Horseman.
Sailor.
Steward on Steamboat.
Switchman.
Stevedore.
Slater.
Steel Polisher.
Telegraph Builder.
Timber Cutter.
Train Starter.
Wood Carver and Turner.
Yard Master.

CLASS III.

Agricultural Implement Maker.
Bar Keeper.
Blacksmith (working).
Blast Furnace (working in).
Block, Oar and Mast Maker
Boiler Maker.
Bolt Maker.
Brass Founder (working).
Bricklayer.
Broker in Cattle and Horses.
Baggage Master on Trains.
Baggage Master at Station.
Canal Boatman.
Captain on River Steamer.
Car Driver.
Carman (Drayman).
Carpenter and Joiner.
Caulker (Ship).
Coachman.
Cork Cutter.
Cooper.
Coal Heaver.
Carpenter (Railroad).
Chief Engineer.
Car Repairer.
Car Cleaner.
Conductor on Passenger Trains.
Distiller.
Driver of Express Wagon.
Drover.
Detective (Railroad).
Express Agent (not on trains).
Express Agent on trains.
Engineer on Stationary Engine.
Express Messenger on Trains.
Foundry (employee in).
Fireman (Engine, Hose, Hook and Ladder).
Freight Agent (station).
Freight Laborer.
Hod Carrier.
Horse Breaker.
Hostler.

Inspector of Wood and Timber.
Knife and Instrument Maker.
Lead Pipe and Tube Maker.
Lighthouse or Lightship Keeper.
Lightning Rods (one who puts up).
Livery Stable Keeper.
Lumberman, manufacturer.
Laborer, common.
Locomotive Superintendent.
Limestone Quarrier or Burner.
Master Mechanic.
Mason.
Machinist.
Metal Turner.
Miner (surface).
Naval Architect.
Operative in Saw and Planing Mills.
Painter.
Prison Office Keeper.
Puddler.
Rolling Mills
Saw Mill (employee).
Shooting Gallery Keeper.
Scythe and Sickle Maker.
Ship Carpenter.
Shipsmith.
Slate Quarrier.
Stable Keeper.
Stage Driver.
Sugar Refinery (workman in)
Station man.
Signal man.
Ship Inspector.
Stone Cutter and Dresser.
Track Laborer.
Track Superintendent.
Track Foreman.
Track Inspector.
Teamster.
Turpentine Manufacturer.
Watchman.
Wood Chopper.

CLASS IV.

Actor, Actress.
Ale or Beer Manufacturer.
Apothecary, Druggist.
Architect.
Armorer.
Artificial Limb Maker.
Actuary.
Artist, Painter.
Attorney, Lawyer.
Auditor.
Army or Navy Officer (not in service).
Author, Writer.
Bookseller.
Broker in mdse., stocks, or gold.
Bank Officer or Clerk.
Book-keeper, Accountant.
Baker.
Barber.
Basket-maker.
Bell-hanger.
Boat Builder.
Bookbinder.
Boot and Shoe Maker.
Box and Trunk Maker.
Brass Polisher, Finisher.
Brewer.
Brickmaker.
Builder, not Laborer
Cabinet Maker.

Cap or Carpet-bag Maker.
Carpet Weaver.
Chair Maker.
Chemist and Druggist.
Chiropodist.
Civil Engineer.
Clock Maker.
Coach Maker.
Coffee-House Keeper.
Commercial Agent.
Clergyman. Minister.
Clerk, (generally).
Clothier.
Commission Merchant.
Captain of lake or sea steamer.
Chemist, manufacturing.
Coal Miner (underground).
Confectioner.
Cook (professional).
Coppersmith
Copperplate Printer.
Cornice Moulder.
Cotton Dyer.
Cotton Packer and Presser.
Cotton Printer.
Cow-keeper, Milk Seller.
Currier
Custom house Officer.
Cut

CLASS IV —*Concluded.*

Draughtsman.
Dressmaker.
Dentist.
Die Engraver, Mould Maker.
Drug Grinder.
Eating-House Keeper.
Embosser.
Embroiderer.
Engraver.
Editor, Reporter.
Engineer, Mining.
Fisherman.
Farmer, owner.
Farm Laborer.
File Maker.
Fish Curer.
Fish and Oyster Dealer.
Furrier.
Gardener.
Gas Fitter.
Gas Works, service.
Gauger.
General Trader, (traveling).
Glazier.
Glover.
Gold Beater.
Glass Blower.
Gold or Silver Refiner and Worker.
Grocer (general).
Grain Measurer.
General Trader, storekeeper.
Grave Digger, Sexton.
Gunsmith.
Harness Maker, Saddler.
Hat and Cap Maker.
Hollow Ware Maker.
Hoop Maker.
Hoop Skirt Maker.
Hotel or Tavern Keeper (country).
House Decorator.
Huckster.
Hotel Keeper, proprietor.
Insurance Officer and Clerks (not travelling).
Ivory Cutter and Worker.
India Rubber Manufactory, employee in.
Ink Maker.
Instrument Case Maker.
Japanner.
Jeweler, worker.
Lithographer (not working).
Leather Dyer.
Locksmith.
Looking Glass Maker.
Last Maker.
Machinist, not in employ of railroad.
Marble Cutter.
Marble Mason.
Marketman.
Medical Student.
Metal Refiner.
Miller, grain and flour.
Morocco Dresser.
Millwright.
Manufacturer (not working).
Milliner.
Musician.
Moulder.
Naval Officer, in service.
Nail Maker.
Nurseryman, working.
Oil Dealer, petroleum.
Operative in Cotton or Woolen Mills.
Organ Builder.
Oyster Dealer.
Phonographer.
Photographer.
Physician.
Postmaster.
P. O. Clerk (not traveling)
Packer of Hay, Cotton, Pork, Beef.
Packing Case Maker (not using circular saw).
Painter, house, ornamental.
Paper Hanger.
Paper Box Maker.
Pastry Cook.
Pawnbroker.
Pencil Maker.
Picture frame Maker.
Percussion Cap Maker.
Plasterer.
Plater.
Plumber.
Porter.
Potter.
Pressman.
Printer, compositor.
Pump Maker.
President or Secretary of Corporation
Publisher.
Purser, steamship.
Policeman.
Railroad Employees.
Rectifier.
Rope Maker.
Surgeon.
Ship Rigger.
Soap Boiler.
Sail Maker.
Saloon Keeper.
Sausage Maker.
Segar Maker.
Scourer, Dyer.
Ship Broker, agent.
Ship Builder, contractor.
Steward on vessel or steamer.
Smelter.
Soda Water Manufacturer.
Shovel Maker.
Silversmith.
Spindle Maker.
Spring Maker.
Steel Pen Maker.
Stereotyper.
Surgical Instrument Maker.
Surveyor.
Tanner.
Tinman, tinker.
Traveling Agent.
Type Founder.
Tailor.
Teacher.
Telegraph Operator.
Tool Maker.
Turner, Wood and Ivory
Umbrella Maker.
Upholsterer.
Varnish Maker.
Vitriol Manufacturer.
Watchmaker.
Weighing Machine, Scale Maker.
Wharfinger.
Wheelwright.
Whip Maker.
Whitesmith.
Wig Maker.
Wire Maker.
Wood Dealer
Watchman.
Weaver.
Weigher.

Note to page 16.

The popular idea that the affection known as "clergyman's sore throat" predisposes to consumption is, to a great extent, erroneous. On the other hand, it is probably safe to say that consumption finds fewer victims among the clergy, than among any other class of people—the exercise of public speaking tending rather to develope and strengthen the lungs than otherwise. As a general rule, public speakers are safe and desirable risks.

Note to page 16. (Professional men.)

It must be admitted, as an exception to the general rule, that under-teachers in city schools are most unfavorably situated as regards health and longevity. Confined for six or eight hours a day in close, ill-ventilated rooms, which are crowded with children in all stages of uncleanliness; with both body and mind wrought up to the highest pitch of exertion, and all this for many consecutive weeks or even months, it is scarcely to be wondered at that their standard of health is low as compared with that of the great majority of teachers in the colleges and higher schools, or of teachers in common schools in country towns.

It is probable that statistics would show a marked difference in the average duration of life, between city and country physicians, and that the difference would be in favor of the former. The terribly exhausting life of the country practitioner, together with his unavoidable irregularity of habits and of hours of rest, cannot be otherwise than unfavorable to long life.

As regards other professions, it does not appear that any marked difference obtains between city and country. But the popular belief, that the opportunities for the enjoyment of vigorous health, are, on the whole, better in the country than in the city, is probably true, though a series of observations on this point are much needed. The actual difference, however, is not so great as has been supposed; owing perhaps to the increasing popularity of gymnastic and other exercises intended to develop a high state of physical health; the improved methods of constructing dwelling houses as regards warming and ventilation, and the improved notions of society as regards diet and dress; fashionable society having now learned to tolerate *warm* attire, however ridiculous or preposterous its *form* may be—another reason for the improved hygienic condition of cities is, that modern science has at length developed the fact that contagious and zymotic diseases may be, to a great extent, prevented by the enforcement of sanitary regulations; consequently every city of any considerable size has its "Board of Health," clothed with ample powers, and held rigidly accountable for their employment, both by public opinion, and by an exacting and critical newspaper press.

Note to page 19. (Table of Mortality.)
In the first of the annexed tables, is shown the mortality from all diseases usually mentioned in Life Insurance Applications, for the year 1860, together with the rates they severally bear to 10,000 deaths, from all known causes of mortality. The second table shows the proportion of deaths to 10,000 from all causes, in the several "census districts" of the United States, from the same diseases, and for the same year. The States and Territories comprising the several districts will be found in connection with the table on page 16. It will be observed that the deaths from "colic," "palpitation" and "spitting of blood" are not given; this is simply because they are very properly regarded as being *symptoms* only; and therefore entitled to no place in a classified arrangement of diseases for scientific purposes. (Compiled from the Census Report for 1860).

As Life Insurance Companies have multiplied, and operations on a more extended scale have been made, tables of mortality have also multiplied.

The Carlisle table is given on page 7, of this work; below will be found the "American," "Combined Experience" and "English" tables—the latter being that generally known as "Farr's table."

SHOWING THE DEATHS IN THE UNITED STATES, AND THE RATIO TO 10,000 DEATHS, FROM DISEASES USUALLY MENTIONED IN LIFE INSURANCE APPLICATIONS, FOR THE YEAR 1860.

DISEASE.	NO. OF DEATHS.	NO. TO 10,000 FROM ALL KNOWN CAUSES.	DISEASE.	NO. OF DEATHS.	NO. TO 10,000 FROM ALL KNOWN CAUSES.
Apoplexy	3,083	86	Insanity	452	12
Asthma	669	18	Influenza	385	10
Bronchitis	1,919	53	Liver Complaint	2,633	73
Cancer	3,292	92	Paralysis	4,637	130
Consumption	49,082	1,379	Palpitation		
Colic	44	1	Quinsy	730	20
Diphtheria	1,663	46	Rheumatism	1,881	52
Disease of the Heart	6,530	183	Rupture	360	10
Dropsy	12,090	355	Scarlet Fever	26,402	741
Fits (Epileptic)	501	14	Spitting of Blood		
Fistula	37	1	Disease of Urinary Organs	2,112	56
Gout	41	1	Syphilis	233	6
Intemperance	931	26			

SHOWING THE PROPORTION OF DEATHS TO 10,000 FROM ALL CAUSES, IN THE "CENSUS DISTRICTS" FOR THE YEAR 1860.

DISEASE.	DISTRICTS. PROPORTION TO 10,000 OF ALL DEATHS.								
	I.	II.	III.	IV.	V.	VI.	VII.	VIII.	IX.
Apoplexy	109	84	141	62	78	55	86	63	110
Asthma	17	16	25	15	26	9	29	14	37
Bronchitis	31	18	115	46	60	65	62	48	51
Cancer	140	81	107	79	95	60	71	50	47
Consumption	2,162	1,535	1,793	1,298	1,195	1,048	492	563	1,214
Colic									
Diphtheria	47	4	73	30	81	35	20	52	116
Disease of the Heart	319	135	236	126	164	95	96	83	215
Dropsy	314	286	369	258	507	314	601	329	241
Fits (Eliptic)	17	22	18	14	8	12	12	7	15
Fistula	1					2		1	5
Gout		2	1		3				1
Intemperance	23	22	22	15	39	30	29	27	73
Insanity	18	9	16	7	13	11	8	9	11
Influenza	15	7	4	6	8	7	17	14	7
Liver Complaint	81	107	74	74	73	61	74	51	102
Paralysis	177	75	194	103	190	88	99	44	92
Palpitation									
Quinsy	3	12	8	18	19	31	42	48	11
Rheumatism	46	45	52	45	75	59	62	43	59
Rupture	68	13	11	9	14	9	8	9	19
Scarlet Fever	766	1,093	1,085	1,112	380	766	198	374	965
Spitting of Blood									
Disease of the Urinary Organs	82	55	57	52	60	49	54	35	59
Syphilis	7	51	3	3	4	5	11	7	51

RATES OF ENGLISH AND AMERICAN MORTALITY.

Age.	American Table. Number Living.	Combined Experience. Number living.	American Table. Number Dying.	Combined Experience. Number dying.	American Table. Expectation of Life.	Combined Experience. Expectation of Life.	English Life Table No. 3, (males). Expectation of Life.
10	100,000	100,000	749	676	48.72	48.36	47.05
11	99,251	99,324	746	674	48.08	47.68	46.31
12	98,505	98,650	743	672	47.44	47.01	45.54
13	97,762	97,978	740	671	46.82	46.33	44.76
14	97,022	97,307	737	671	46.16	45.64	43.97
15	96,285	96,636	735	671	45.50	44.96	43.18
16	95,550	95,965	732	672	44.85	44.27	42.40
17	94,818	95,293	729	673	44.19	43.58	41.64
18	94,089	94,620	727	675	43.53	42.88	40.90
19	93,362	93,945	725	677	42.87	42.19	40.17
20	92,637	93,268	723	680	42.20	41.49	39.48
21	91,914	92,588	722	683	41.53	40.79	38.80
22	91,192	91,905	721	686	40.85	40.09	38.13
23	90,471	91,219	720	690	40.17	39.39	37.46
24	89,751	90,529	719	694	39.49	38.68	36.79
25	89,032	89,835	718	698	38.81	37.98	36.12
26	88,314	89,137	718	703	38.11	37.27	35.44
27	87,596	88,434	718	708	37.43	36.56	34.77
28	86,878	87,726	718	714	36.73	35.86	34.10
29	86,160	87,012	719	720	36.03	35.15	33.43
30	85,441	86,292	720	727	35.33	34.43	32.76
31	84,721	85,565	721	734	34.62	33.72	32.09
32	84,000	84,831	723	742	33.92	33.01	31.42
33	83,277	84,089	726	750	33.21	32.30	30.74
34	82,551	83,339	729	758	32.50	31.58	30.07
35	81,822	82,581	732	767	31.78	30.87	29.40
36	81,090	81,814	737	776	31.07	30.15	28.73
37	80,353	81,038	742	785	30.35	29.44	28.06
38	79,611	80,253	749	795	29.62	28.72	27.39
39	78,862	79,458	756	805	28.90	28.00	26.72
40	78,106	78,653	765	815	28.18	27.28	26.06
41	77,341	77,838	774	826	27.45	26.56	25.39
42	76,567	77,012	785	839	26.72	25.84	24.73
43	75,782	76,173	797	857	25.99	25.12	24.07
44	74,985	75,316	812	881	25.27	24.40	23.41
45	74,173	74,435	828	909	24.54	23.69	22.76
46	73,345	73,526	848	944	23.80	22.97	22.11
47	72,497	72,582	870	981	23.08	22.27	21.46
48	71,627	71,601	896	1,021	22.36	21.56	20.82
49	70,731	70,580	927	1,063	21.63	20.87	20.17
50	69,804	69,517	962	1,108	20.91	20.18	19.54
51	68,842	68,409	1,001	1,156	20.20	19.50	18.90
52	67,841	67,253	1,044	1,207	19.49	18.82	18.28

RATES OF ENGLISH AND AMERICAN MORTALITY.

Age.	American Table. Number Living.	Combined Experience. Number living.	American Table. Number Dying.	Combined Experience. Number dying.	American Table. Expectation of Life.	Combined Experience. Expectation of Life.	English Life Table No. 3 (males). Expectation of Life.
53	66,797	66,046	1,091	1,261	18.79	18.16	17.67
54	65,706	64,785	1,143	1,316	18.09	17.50	17.06
55	64,563	63,469	1,199	1,375	17.40	16.86	16.45
56	63,364	62,094	1,260	1,436	16.72	16.22	15.86
57	62,104	60,658	1,325	1,497	16.05	15.59	15.26
58	60,779	59,161	1,394	1,561	15.39	14.97	14.68
59	59,385	57,600	1,468	1,627	14.74	14.37	14.10
60	57,917	55,973	1,546	1,698	14.09	13.77	13.53
61	56,371	54,275	1,628	1,770	13.47	13.18	12.96
62	54,743	52,505	1,713	1,844	12.86	12.61	12.41
63	53,030	50,661	1,800	1,917	12.26	12.05	11.87
64	51,230	48,744	1,889	1,990	11.68	11.51	11.34
65	49,341	46,754	1,980	2,061	11.10	10.97	10.82
66	47,361	44,693	2,070	2,128	10.54	10.46	10.32
67	45,291	42,565	2,158	2,191	10.00	9.96	9.83
68	43,133	40,374	2,243	2,246	9.48	9.47	9.36
69	40,890	38,128	2,321	2,291	8.98	9.00	8.90
70	38,569	35,837	2,391	2,327	8.48	8.54	8.45
71	36,178	33,510	2,448	2,351	8.00	8.10	8.03
72	33,730	31,159	2,487	2,362	7.54	7.67	7.62
73	31,243	28,797	2,505	2,358	7.10	7.26	7.22
74	28,738	26,439	2,501	2,339	6.68	6.86	6.85
75	26,237	24,100	2,476	2,303	6.28	6.48	6.49
76	23,761	21,797	2,431	2,249	5.88	6.11	6.15
77	21,330	19,548	2,369	2,179	5.48	5.76	5.82
78	18,961	17,369	2,291	2,092	5.10	5.42	5.51
79	16,670	15,277	2,196	1,987	4.74	5.09	5.21
80	14,474	13,290	2,091	1,866	4.38	4.78	4.93
81	12,383	11,424	1,964	1,730	4.04	4.48	4.66
82	10,419	9,694	1,816	1,582	3.71	4.18	4.41
83	8,603	8,112	1,648	1,427	3.39	3.90	4.17
84	6,955	6,685	1,470	1,268	3.08	3.63	3.95
85	5,485	5,417	1,292	1,111	2.77	3.36	3.73
86	4,193	4,306	1,114	958	2.47	3.10	3.53
87	3,079	3,348	933	811	2.19	2.84	3.34
88	2,146	2,537	744	673	1.93	2.59	3.16
89	1,402	1,864	555	545	1.69	2.35	3.00
90	847	1,319	385	427	1.42	2.11	2.84
91	462	892	246	322	1.19	1.89	2.69
92	216	570	137	231	98	1.67	2.55
93	79	339	58	155	80	1.47	2.41
94	21	184	18	95	64	1.28	2.29
95	3	89	3	52	50	1.12	2.17

The following simple rules for the calculation of life expectation are taken from the "Agents Manual of Life Insurance." They may be relied upon as approximately correct, and will be found useful in the absence of the standard mortality tables:

From 14 to 26 inclusive, deduct the age from 100; half the balance is the expectation
" 26 to 30   "   "   "   "   98   "   "   "   "
" 31 to 40   "   "   "   "   96   "   "   "   "
" 41 to 50   "   "   "   "   92   "   "   "   "
" 51 to 60   "   "   "   "   90   "   "   "   "

Or deduct the age of the party, whatever it may be, from 80, and two-thirds of the difference is the average expectation; for example, if the age be 43; 80—43=37; $\frac{2}{3}$ of 37=24$\frac{2}{3}$, the average expectation, very nearly, as given by the table.

The annexed table, after Quetelet, shows the relative mortality of the sexes, at different ages from birth up to 100 years, as affected by city and country life. The table is constructed to exhibit the proportion of male deaths to one female death, in both localities.

TABLE SHOWING THE RELATIVE MORTALITY OF THE SEXES AT DIFFERENT AGES IN CITY AND COUNTRY.—(AFTER QUETELET).

Age.	Male Deaths to 1 Female Death.	
	City.	Country.
Still born	1.33	1.70
0 to 1 month	1.33	1.37
1 to 2 months	1.37	1.2
2 to 3 months	1.22	1.21
3 to 6 months	1.24	1.16
6 to 12 months	1.06	1.03
1 to 2 years	1.06	0.97
2 to 5 years	1.	0.94
5 to 14 years	0.9	0.92
14 to 18 years	0.82	0.75
18 to 21 years	0.98	0.92
21 to 26 years	1.24	1.11
26 to 30 years	1.00	0.86
30 to 40 years	0.88	0.63
40 to 50 years	1.02	0.83
50 to 60 years	1.07	1.18
60 to 70 years	0.96	1.05
70 to 80 years	0.77	1.00
80 to 100 years	0.68	0.92

The comparative mortality of the white and colored races is a subject of practical and growing importance in its relations to Life Insurance. Already the blacks are beginning to show an intelligent appreciation of the benefits of Life Insurance, and the time is not far distant when it will become quite general among them. Full and reliable statistical information in regard to the average duration of life among them is not yet accessible : but the following tables, whereof the first is compiled from the Census Report of 1860, and the two following from that excellent authority, Dr. W. A. Hammond, are believed to be reliable, so far as they go.

Table first, shows the comparative mortality of whites and blacks in the United States, from diseases alluded to in the applications of the various companies ; the second, shows the comparative mortality of whites and blacks from consumption, at several of the British military stations, as it occurs from year to year ; the third, shows the comparative mortality from malarial diseases at the same stations, (Gibraltar excepted) from 1818 to 1836 inclusive.

SHOWING THE COMPARATIVE MORTALITY OF WHITES AND BLACKS IN THE UNITED STATES, FROM DISEASES MENTIONED IN THE LIFE INSURANCE APPLICATIONS, FOR THE YEAR 1850

	NUMBER OF DEATHS.		RATIO IN 100,000 DEATHS.	
Causes of Death.	White.	Colored.	White.	Colored.
Apoplexy............................	10.184	944	18.691	10.107
Asthma.............................	926	258	1.699	2.762
Bronchitis.........................	6.722	2.094	12.337	22.420
Cancer..............................	3.179	346	5.834	3.704
Consumption.....................	70.893	7.771	130.117	83.203
Colic................................	....	....	....	....
Diphtheria........................	1.529	09	2.806	96
Diseases of the Heart.........	7.662	849	14.062	9.000
Dropsy.............................	13.891	4.766	25.495	51.029
Fits, (Epileptic).................	1.074	202	1.971	2.162
Fistula.............................	26	07	47	74
Gout................................	79	05	144	53
Intemperance....................	1.792	177	3.289	1.895
Insanity...........................	574	91	1.053	974
Influenza..........................	341	144	625	1.541
Liver Complaint................	3.211	294	5.893	3.147
Paralysis..........................	....	....	....	....
Palpitation.......................	....	....	....	....
Quinsy.............................	1.284	313	2.356	3.351
Rheumatism.....................	1.500	363	2.753	3.886
Rupture...........................	367	149	673	1.695
Scarlet Fever....................	23.721	1.681	43.537	17.998
Spitting of Blood...............	....	....	....	....
Diseases of Urinary Organs	3.308	276	6.065	2.972
Syphilis............................	657	149	1.207	1.595

NOTE.—The blank spaces indicate that the diseases opposite them are regarded as *symptoms* merely

TABLE SHOWING THE COMPARATIVE MORTALITY OF WHITE AND BLACK TROOPS FROM CONSUMPTION AT SEVERAL OF THE BRITISH MILITARY STATIONS, AS IT OCCURS FROM YEAR TO YEAR.—(From Hammond).

Station.	RATIO OF DEATHS IN 1,000.	
	White Troops.	Colored Troops.
Jamaica	7.5	10.3
Bahama Islands	6.	9.7
Honduras	3.	8.1
Sierra Leone	6.	6.3
Mauritius	4.	12.9
Ceylon	4.9	10.5
Gibralter	5.3	43.

TABLE SHOWING THE COMPARATIVE MORTALITY FROM MALARIAL DISEASES, OF WHITE AND BLACK TROOPS, AT THE SAME STATIONS, FROM 1818 TO 1836.—(From Hammond.)

Station.	RATIO OF DEATHS TO 1,000.	
	White Troops.	Colored Troops.
Jamaica	101.9	8.2
Bahama Islands	15.9	5.6
Honduras	81.	4.4
Sierra Leone	410.	2.4
Mauritius	1.7	0.0
Ceylon	24.6	1.1

Note to page 22. (Intemperance.)

That intemperance, using the term in its largest sense, sometimes seems to be hereditary, is undeniably true. The morbid appetite seems, after long indulgence, to become a fixed constitutional vice, and as such to be handed down from father to son. Yet it is frequently the case that the children of an intemperate man, smarting under the disgrace of having a besotted father, become, from very disgust and loathing, the most radical temperance men; but *their* children are more than likely to follow the course of their grandparent Indeed, in intemperate families, "atavism" is a common occurrence, and is explicable on the grounds above stated. When an applicant comes of a family known to have been intemperate for two or more generations past, his habits should be most carefully scrutinized by the Examiner, before recommending him.

Note to page 23. (Alcohol.)

Reformed inebriates, unless after a long interval of sobriety, are undesirable; the long-continued and excessive use of alcohol leaving behind effects more or less permanent in their nature. "The characteristic changes which have been observed in the brain, *medulla oblongata, etc.*, of confirmed drinkers,"—writes Mr. Anstie—"consist essentially of a peculiar atrophic modification, by which the true elements of nervous tissue are partially removed, the total mass of nervous matter wastes, serous fluid is effused into the ventricles and the arachnoid, while simultaneously there is a marked development of fibrous tissue, granular fat and other elements which belong to a lower order of vitalized products." Moreover, intemperance is a recognized cause of insanity, particularly if any hereditary predisposition thereto exists: out of 816 cases of insanity, treated in a well-known eastern asylum, 55, or one in about every 15, were directly traceable to excessive use of alcohol.

Note to page 25. (Acclimation.)

The progeny of parents of northern extraction, born in the tropics, even though sent to a temperate zone early in life, are often questionable risks. The enervating influences of a tropical climate seems to follow them through all their lives; seems indeed, in a single generation, ofttimes to so modify and break down the constitution, as to render it incapable of long resisting the depressing influences of a northern climate. This is best exemplified in the children of missionaries, born of parents who have for several—or perhaps many—years resided in the tropical missionary fields, and who have been sent early in life to the United States to be educated. Very many such instances occur in New England, from whence most of the missionaries to eastern countries have, until recently, been drawn; and whither their children are often sent, to be reared and educated among relatives. Experience has fully demonstrated the fact, that these children born in the tropics fall an easy prey to consumption, or some one of the more virulent zymotic diseases, before arriving at mature years. If, however, the period of maturity has been safely reached and passed, and if the risk seems safe and desirable in other regards, the mere fact of having been born in the tropics need not of necessity reject. But in the general make-up of the risk, it must not be overlooked, or treated as an item of no importance in its relations to longevity.

Note to pages 29 and 115.

The ready return of chronic camp diarrhœa, even after a long period of *apparent* perfect recovery, suggests great caution; it is, however, true, that the lapse of time diminishes the liability to a return of the disease.

Within the past year, camp diarrhœa has in a great measure disappeared; and, in our own experience, cases applying for treatment have proved much less obstinate than they were during and immediately after the war—a return to home comforts and the habits of civil life proving, in the great majority of instances, sufficient to bring about a perfect recovery. Indeed, we may reasonably expect that, in a few years hence, this fearful scourge will only be known historically. But unless the bowels have been in a healthy condition for a long period—certainly not less than a year—the risk should be declined.

Note to pages 32 and 88. (Consumption.)

The well-known hereditary character of consumption is always to be borne in mind; but it does not therefore follow, that every applicant, one of whose parents died of consumption, is uninsurable. The opinion seems to be gaining ground, especially in England, that the proportion of non-hereditary cases of this disease, is much larger than has been supposed. "That the tuberculous constitution"—says Dr. Aitken—"is transmitted from parent to child, has long been a popular belief, and regarded as one of the best established points in the etiology of the disease. Actual *proof*, however, has never yet been afforded of the justness of the general conviction. Out of 102 phthisical patients admitted into Brompton Hospital, for Consumption, 26 per cent. came of tuberculous parents, "a circumstance which may be predicated of any mass of individuals taken in a hospital: namely, that 26 per cent. of them are of phthisical parents" On the other hand, while the general statement may be made, that some cases of phthisis may be traced to hereditary influence, "it is undoubted that much *phthisis is in each generation non-hereditary.*" Our present limits do not permit a lengthy discussion of this topic: but the following conclusions seem to the writer, warranted by past experience.

First. Where both parents have died of consumption, the risk should *invariably* be rejected.

Secondly. If brothers or sisters of the applicant have died of the same disease, the risk is rendered less desirable.

Thirdly. A risk, otherwise desirable, need not be rejected because the party's mother died of consumption; but, if the party has not already and safely passed the age at or about which the mother was attacked, extreme caution should be exercised in the acceptance of the risk.

The annexed table shows the ratio of deaths from consumption to 10,000 deaths from all causes, in the several census districts of the United States for the year 1860; and the same as modified by sex. (Compiled from the Census Report.)

DISTRICTS.	RATIO TO TOTAL DEATHS.		RATIO OF SEXES.	
	MALE.	FEMALE.	MALE.	FEMALE.
DISTRICT 1.—Maine, New Hampshire, Vermont, Massachusetts, Rhode Island, Connecticut and New York.....	1,922	2,419	1,000	1.258
DISTRICT 2.—Michigan, Wisconsin, Minnesota and Nebraska.................	1,323	1,780	1,000	1,345
DISTRICT 3.—New Jersey and Pennsylvania....................................	1,700	1,901	1,000	1,123
DISTRICT 4.—Ohio, Indiana, Illinois, Iowa and Kansas........................	1,182	1,427	1,000	1,207
DISTRICT 5.—Delaware, Maryland, District of Columbia, Virginia and North Carolina.............................	1,004	1,391	1,000	1,378
DISTRICT 6.—Kentucky, Tennessee and Missouri...	871	1,245	1,000	1,425
DISTRICT 7.—South Carolina, Georgia, Florida and Alabama................	402	591	1,000	1,470
DISTRICT 8.—Mississippi, Louisiana, Arkansas and Texas......................	550	583	1,000	1,060
DISTRICT 9.—Oregon, California, Dakota, New Mexico, Utah and Washington	1,258	1,136	1,000	902

Note to page 32.

Mere Nephralgia should be diagnosticated as comparatively unimportant; but it is probable that, in the great majority of instances, nephralgia is symptomatic of the passage of a calculus—and is therefore warrant for rejection, or at least a suspension of judgment. Nephralgia is also, occasionally, the expression of malarial irritation —in which case it is no obstacle to insurance.

Note to pages 37 and 137. (Insanity.)

Probably in no disease, liable to present itself to the Examiner, is the hereditary tendency more strongly or more uniformly marked, than in insanity. Out of 1,654 cases admitted into the Hartford "Retreat for the Insane," 304, or about one in every five cases, were of hereditary origin. Dr. Aitken gives the ratio as "varying from 26 to 69 per cent." It is also important to bear in mind that hereditary insanity is prone to assume the most hopeless and incurable form of this disease; namely "Melancholia:" of fifteen cases investigated by the writer, *all* were clearly hereditary. But there is still another point to which the attention of the Insurance Examiner should be drawn: namely, that the suicidal propensity is more strongly marked in Melancholia than in any other form of the disease.

The Diagnosis of some forms of "delusional" insanity is sometimes exceedingly difficult. The following rules, copied from Aitken, as compiled by him from the admirable work of Bucknill & Tuke, are practically valuable:

(1.) Learn as thoroughly as possible the antecedents and history of the patient.

(2.) Estimate the value of the hereditary tendency, upon the following principles: (A.) The insanity of one parent indicates a less degree of predisposition than that of a parent and an uncle; and still less than that of a parent and a grand-parent, or of two parents. (B.) The insanity of a parent and a grand-parent, with an uncle or an aunt in the same line, may be held to indicate even stronger predisposition than the insanity of both parents. (C.) The insanity of a parent occurring after the birth of a child, without predisposition, is of no value in the formation of an hereditary tendency. (D.) If several brothers or sisters, older and younger than the patient, [or applicant,] have become insane, the fact tells strongly in favor of predisposition, although neither parent nor grand-parent may have been lunatic. (E.) The insanity of cousins cannot yet be determined as worth anything in favor of predisposition, except in corroboration of other and weightier facts.

(3.) Ascertain if there has been any change of habits or predisposition.

(4.) Exercise the greatest tact and discretion in the personal examination of probably insane patients.

(5.) Observe any peculiarities of residence or dress.

(6.) Study the appearances, demeanor, and general conduct of the patient.

(7.) Notice any peculiarities of bodily condition; [as emaciation, state of the skin, bowels, pulse, tongue, etc.]

(8.) Observe any peculiarities of gesture, or of countenance.

As a general rule, when, upon close examination, insanity appears to be clearly hereditary—and especially if the parent whose sex agrees with that of the party under examination became insane before his or her birth, the risk had better be declined, even though it may be in other respects desirable.

Note to page 40. (Palpitation.)

The following list includes the chief causes of palpitation of the heart, except when dependent upon organic disease of the organ itself: (1.) Diseases or derangements of remote organs, as the stomach or liver. (2.) The use of narcotics or stimulants, as alcohol, opium, or tobacco. (3.) Gouty, rheumatic or malarial irritation. (4,) Masturbation, or excessive sexual indulgence. (5.) Excessive or prolonged mental labor. (6,) Hysteria, disordered menstruation. (7.) Anæmia or leucocythæmia.

In the latter case it will probably be associated with cardiac, as well as arterial and venous murmurs; the former best heard over the base of the heart, and the latter along the course of the carotids. Whenever these are present, the risk must be declined: *First*, because the anæmia is of itself sufficient cause for rejection; and, *Secondly*, because it is impossible to distinguish with absolute certainty between the sounds caused by the watery condition of the blood, and those caused by actual organic disease. Palpitation is also occasionally associated with, and dependent upon spinal irritation, "especially if there is tenderness of the upper half of the spine." When easily excited, or long continued, it is very liable to result in organic disease of the heart—and is *certainly* indicative of some source of trouble, which it should be the business of the Examiner to ferret out and explain, before recommending the risk.

Note to page 46. (Spitting of Blood.)

While the expectoration of blood is, with great propriety, generally looked upon as an insuperable obstacle to insurance, it is, of course, *possible* that a person, who is exceedingly desirable as an insurance risk, may have sometime spat blood from the mouth; for example, the bloody expectoration of acute bronchitis, or of pneumonia, by no means precludes the idea of subsequent vigorous health, and therefore of insurability—and justice to the applicant demands that the cause be carefully sought out. But whenever a *doubt* exists, that fact alone should determine the rejection of the risk—else would the examiner impair rather than increase the safety of the company employing him.

In insurance applications, the term "spitting of blood" is of course used arbitrarily, else would almost every applicant who answers this question negatively perjure himself. It is intended to ascertain whether any expectoration of blood from the lungs or bronchial tubes, or from any source indicative of organic disease has ever occurred; and it is sometimes necessary to explain to the applicant its scope and meaning. Every man who has had a tooth extracted must have discharged blood from the mouth, and many other causes equally trivial might give rise to the same thing; but while this would, of course, be literally and undeniably "spitting of blood," it would not come within the limits of the technical meaning of this phrase as employed in insurance applications or medical text works. It would be better if the term, on account of its loose and unmeaning phraseology, and on account of its being so frequently and easily misunderstood, could be dropped entirely, and another of greater accuracy substituted for it

The following table is intended to show the more common and dangerous sources of bloody expectoration, together with their prominent symptoms and insurance significance:

SOURCE.	DIAGNOSIS.	CAUSE AND SIGNIFICANCE.
NOSE.	Blood generally issues from the nostrils; sometimes flows backwards, and is coughed up, but if the patient is made to lean forward, the blood flows from the nostrils, which establishes the diagnosis. The blood can generally be seen trickling down the pharynx; and is not usually florid.	Causes are almost always easily made out, and are of little importance to the Insurance Examiner.
MOUTH.	The soft, spongy, swollen state of the gums, with blood slowly oozing from them, and the readiness with which they bleed upon being touched, at once indicates the source.	Generally indicates an impoverished condition of the blood, as in Scorbutus; and calls for great caution.
BRONCHIAL TUBES.	Expectoration consists of mucus or muco-pus, *streaked* with blood, not intimately and uniformly mixed; quantity of blood generally quite small; large, course rales are easily heard.	Acute or chronic bronchitis; foreign bodies, or ulceration are the common causes. Either of these *reject* or suspend until complete recovery takes place.
LUNGS.	Coincident with other signs and symptoms of phthisis; blood in considerable quantity; florid; generally "frothy," or containing small air bubbles, and intimately mixed with muco-pus; not coagulated.	Almost always indicative of tubercular deposit, and is of course an unqualified warrant for rejection.
STOMACH.	Sense of weight and uneasiness in the epigastric region; or perhaps decided nausea; the matter vomited consists of dark grumous blood, altered by the action of gastric juice, unless caused by the opening of an artery, by ulceration; discharges of altered blood from the bowels; tenderness of epigastrium.	Caused by injuries—as a blow or kick; by inflammation or "active hyperæmia"; by ulceration; by cancer; by irritant poisons; by an altered state of the blood itself; or it may be vicarious, as of menstruation. All but the last must of course reject, and *that* even requires careful investigation.

Note to page 48 and 123. (Urine.)

In all cases where symptoms of obscure origin and doubtful significance are present, the urine should be carefully tested by the most approved methods, and, if possible, examined microscopically. Not every Medical Examiner, however, will be so fortunate as to possess a microscope; but no one need be without a supply of test-tubes and reagents, or the skill and knowledge requisite for their use. It is true, however, that, in practice, cases will rarely come before the Examiner in which an examination will either be proper or necessary, and it should never be done when it can safely be avoided; nor should the Examiner *ever* permit himself to subject the applicant to the trouble and annoyance of furnishing him with a specimen of his urine, merely for the purpose of acquiring experience for himself, or of impressing the company employing him with exalted ideas of his scientific ability. Yet cases may and do sometimes arise, when important interests are at stake, and when it becomes the duty of the Examiner to at least make a chemical examination of the urine; in all such cases, the matter should be fully explained to the applicant, that he may understand its necessity and reasonableness. The following table, compiled chiefly from Da Costa and Golding Bird, shows the morbid elements most likely to present themselves to the Insurance Examiner, together with the best means for their detection

MORBID ELEMENT	PHYSICAL CHARACTERS.	TESTS AND REACTIONS.
ALBUMEN.	Sp. gr. varies from 1,010 to 1.025; color light; a precipitate of a light color generally falls after a few hours.	Heat throws down a more or less abundant whitish precipitate, which is insoluble in acid; Nitric acid also precipitates the albumen, and heat fails to re-dissolve it.
BLOOD.	Color red, smoky or dingy; deposits, on standing, a brownish or coffee ground sediment; if in large quantity, minute coagula may be seen at the bottom of the test glass.	The microscope at once reveals the presence of blood globules: Sulph. acid changes the urine to a brown or reddish brown color, showing the presence of hæmatin.

MORBID ELEMENT	PHYSICAL CHARACTERS.	TESTS AND REACTIONS.
SUGAR.	Color light; sp. gr. high; very peculiar odor; rarely deposits sediments; contains large excess of water.	Fill a test tube about one third full of urine; add a few drops of solution of sulphate of copper, or just sufficient to color the urine a light tinge of blue; add liquor potassæ in large excess; the mixture now assumes a deep blue color if sugar be present, and upon being heated, it changes first to a brownish color, then yellow, and finally a reddish brown precipitate of sub-oxide of copper falls to the bottom, which establishes the presence of sugar.
PUS.	When the urine contains pus, it deposits an opaque, creamy sediment, or a gelatinous mass, is generally alkaline and always slightly albuminous.	Upon microscopic examination, pus cells are readily discovered; a drop of acetic acid should be added to the specimen under examination for the purpose of developing the nuclei. The chemical test for pus is liquor potassæ, which forms therewith a gelatinous precipitate of a light straw color.
BILE.	Color very dark; sp. gr. not materially changed; generally coincident with other symptoms of hepatic derangement.	Pour a small quantity of urine on a white plate, or other porcelain surface; a drop of nitric acid is then added; play of color shortly takes place commencing with green an blue, passing to violet and red, and often finally to yellow and brown.
MUCUS.	Color light; a more or less abundant flocculent deposit takes place; putrefactive changes commence very early, the urine rapidly becoming ammoniacal.	Upon the addition of acetic acid, the fluid part of the mucus coagulates into a thin semi-opaque, corrugated membrane, which at once establishes the difference between mucus and pus.

Note to page 76. (Pulse.)

The rapidity of the heart's action is considerably modified by the position of the body; possibly to a greater extent than is commonly supposed. This subject has been carefully studied by Dr. Guy, and with the following results: In 100 healthy males, averaging 27 years of age, in a state of rest, and of freedom from excitement, the average frequency of the pulse was, when standing, 79; when sitting, 70; and when lying, 67 beats per minute;—or a difference of 9 beats between sitting and standing. In 50 healthy females, of the same mean age, and under the same circumstances in other regards, the average pulse when standing, was 89; when sitting, 81; and when lying, 80 beats per minute;—or a difference of 8 beats between standing and sitting.

In my own examinations, I have generally found a difference of from 4 to 8 beats per minute, between the standing and sitting positions; and a difference of less than 6 beats is the rare exception. Yet the difference is very frequently stated, in the reports of Examiners, as being no more than one or two beats—which is, at best, but a very unskillful "guess," and of no value whatever to the company. The pulse should be counted a *full* half minute, *by the watch*, in both positions, and the result should be carefully noted down at the time.

But to the Insurance Examiner, the pulse is, in general, little more than an indication of the condition of the nervous system at the time of the examination. The mere fact that they *are* being examined is sufficient, with many people, to cause a marked acceleration of the heart's action, or even to produce violent palpitation. It is often the case that the applicant has walked rapidly from his place of business to the office of the Examiner, in which case he is almost certain to present an unusually rapid pulse. Many an excellent risk has been needlessly rejected, on account of an unusual rapidity of pulse, which probably subsided before the applicant reached his own home. And this is an act of injustice to both company and applicant. In all cases in which the pulse is merely *rapid*, without symptoms of cardiac or other organic disease, the party should be allowed to sit until the heart shall have had time to resume its normal action; or if this fails of accomplishing the object he should be re-examined on a subsequent occasion, after having learned by experience, that an examination for life insurance is not the fearful ordeal his imagination may have pictured it. I have frequently found it necessary, in my own experience, to make several examinations, and have even found some applicants so exceedingly "nervous" that I have been obliged to resort to the strategy of amusing them for awhile, by cheerful conversation or otherwise, before getting at the *real* character of the heart's action, and have thereby received some most desirable risks which must otherwise have been rejected; and this is precisely the experience of many Medical Examiners. In fact, the pulse is very like an unreliable witness: it must be sharply "cross-examined," before full credence is given to its testimony.

Note to page 127. (Locomotor Ataxy.)

It is by no means impossible that cases of Locomotor Ataxy, in its incipient stage, may present themselves to the Medical Examiner, and its early detection is both very important and very difficult. The symptom first complained of is generally pain, or rather *pains*. The patient generally supposes himself to be troubled with rheumatism or neuralgia ; and careful inquiry will often develop the fact that he has been repeatedly "doctored" for one or the other or both of these diseases. But the anomalous character of these pains ought always to arouse the suspicions of the alert Examiner ; the party describes them as "boring," or "stabbing," or "cutting," or "shooting" pains, and ofttimes seems vainly to rack his brain in search of a word of sufficient force and intensity to express his meaning ; they are generally aggravated by sudden changes of temperature—especially by cold, damp weather; they seldom last longer than from a few seconds to a minute, but are liable to recur at very brief intervals—sometimes as often as "ten, fifteen or twenty times an hour;" they are limited to no particular part of the body, though rather more likely to affect the lower extremities than otherwise. "Often a first sign is reeling about upon getting out of bed in the dark." At this stage, even, while the party admits no deterioration of his general health, careful observation will often detect defective co-ordination: if he is made to walk with his eyes closed, the gait will become unsteady and staggering. Nocturnal incontinence of urine, and nocturnal emissions of semen are also premonitory symptoms of locomotor ataxy; though these are less constant than the peculiar pains and uncertainty of locomotion above alluded to. But when these symptoms are present, the risk should be unhesitatingly declined, and the existence of any one of them suggests great caution, and probably a suspension of judgment.

Note to page 129. (Vertigo.)

Some companies inquire as to previous attacks of vertigo (dizziness). This is a mere symptom, and its true character is usually misapprehended. It is safe to say that it is ordinarily but an evidence of dyspeptic derangement. It is not a precursory symptom of apoplexy, paralysis, or organic diseases of the nervous centre of any sort. (FLINT.) It is *not* an evidence of disease of the heart even. It is sometimes evidence of " nervous asthenia," but under such circumstances concurrent symptoms will readily determine the true character of the case. So also it may occur from sexual excesses, or the inordinate use of tobacco—cessation from the use of narcotics or stimulants, etc. Taken alone, its previous occurrence can scarcely be considered of sufficient importance to materially impair the risk.

Note to page 134. (Softening of the Brain.)

It is unfortunately the case that we have no symptom or group of symptoms which are pathognomonic of softening of the brain in its early stages—the only time at which it is at all liable to come before the Examiner; and this fact gives an additional importance to the disease, in its relation to life insurance.

In the first place, softening of the brain occurs most frequently in those persons whose health has been for some time more or less impaired without any assignable cause being apparent; the symptoms complained of are vague and unmeaning, being indicative of general debility or diminished vital power, rather than of any organic disease; in another class of cases, some "distinct chronic and exhausting disease may be present"—but such cases will rarely or never come before the Insurance Examiner, the evidences of disease being sufficiently marked to attract the attention of the solicitor. The following remarks are intended to apply only to those cases which are "developed slowly and insidiously," and which are *not* preceded by inflammation, hemorrhage, or *acute ramollissement*; in fact to cases of "chronic idiopathic ramollissement," and to these, even, only in their earliest stages. In the great majority of instances, the symptom first attracting attention, is a "torpor and prostration of intellect." The patient himself is generally aware that his powers of mind are gradually becoming weaker and weaker; he finds himself unable to attend to his business—or at least to do so costs him a constant and painful effort; tasks which have seemed to him but trifles heretofore, now assume immense proportions; and he especially laments his inability to undertake and successfully prosecute any task requiring sustained mental effort. Sometimes a sudden inability to prosecute some employment requiring unusual perfection of motor power first excites the patient's alarm; for example, a flutist of celebrity, fifteen months prior to the manifestation of any marked symptoms of cerebral disease, became suddenly unable to "finger" and blow his instrument with his accustomed skill, and this turned out to be a typical case of softening of the brain. "Softening of the cerebral hemispheres," says Andral, "induces alteration in *motion* much more constantly than in intelligence;" but this rule is certainly not without its exceptions; for it is by no means unfrequently the case that memory, or the power of retaining mental impressions and recalling them at will, is one of the early—indeed the earliest—symptoms of cerebral softening. Occasionally the patient notices a slight impairment of the power of controlling the muscles of the lips and tongue, or perhaps of the cheeks and lips, or of the tongue alone; he is surprised to find that he cannot eject his saliva with certainty and accuracy, or that he cannot fix his lips as in the act of whistling; his tongue becomes slightly tremulous, and when protruded turns *slightly* to one side. Another very important symptom, sometimes observed, is an unaccountable inability to write as well as usual; the patient cannot form letters, or guide his pen with accuracy; he complains that "his hand trembles," and calls the attention of his friends to the fact, and to his inability to account for it; words are sometimes spelt wrong, or one word substituted for another. Or the patient sometimes writes and dispatches to distant friends, letters which are but the merest muddle of nonsense—and yet, at this very time, he **may** converse rationally and coherently, and even attend to plain, simple matters of business. Among the prodromic symptoms of softening, may also be mentioned headache, "usually dull in character," numbness, obscure pain, weight or indescribable sensation of "something wrong," in the extremities, a stooping gait, and tendency to cramp in the limbs. When an applicant admits the presence of these symptoms or of any one of them; and especially when to this is super added a general appearance of debility, let the risk be unqualifiedly rejected.

Note to page 144. (Female applicants.)

Extreme longevity is but rarely reached by women; yet the *average* duration of life among women is longer than among men, probably because they are less exposed to causes of mortality—and this even, with the perils incident to maternity added to other causes. In fact other things being equal, the woman who is happily a wife and mother is far preferable, as an insurance risk, to the unfortunate spinster, upon whom age and decrepitude are only too certain to creep prematurely.

The following tables are self-explaining, and therefore require no comment:

TABLE SHOWING THE COMPARATIVE MORTALITY OF FIRST AND SUBSEQUENT LABORS.

Authority.	No. of Primipiræ.	No. of Deaths.	Or one in every	No. of Multipiræ.	No. of Deaths.	Or one in every
Hardy & McClintock	2,125	35	60	4,510	30	150
Matthews Duncan...	3,722	50	74	12,671	103	123
Johnson & Sinclair..	4,535	83	54	9,213	80	115
Totals	10,382	168	62	26,394	213	124

SHOWING THE MORTALITY FROM PUERPERAL FEVER IN DIF-
FERENT PREGNANCIES.—(MATTHEWS DUNCAN.)

No. of Pregnancy.	No. of Mothers.	No. of Deaths.	Percentage of Deaths.	Or one in
First...........................	2,253	97	4.30	23
Second to Fourth...............	4,031	85	2.11	47
Fifth to Ninth..................	1,563	47	3.01	33
Tenth to Nineteenth............	189	9	4.76	21

SHOWING THE RELATIVE LONGEVITY OF MARRIED AND UN-
MARRIED FEMALES.

At the age of—	A married female has to live—		An unmarried female has to live—		Difference.	
	Years.	Months.	Years.	Months.	Years.	Mos
20...............	40	4	30	8	9	8
25...............	36	0	30	6	5	6
30...............	32	5	28	11	3	6
35...............	28	11	26	4	2	7
40...............	25	7	23	5	2	2

From the "Insurance Guide and Hand Book."

Symptoms referable to Tobacco.

Medical examiners, especially in the United States, will meet with many cases presenting symptoms of somewhat obscure origin, which may without doubt, be fairly attributed to the excessive use of tobacco. It is peculiarly prone to disturb the heart's action, rendering its contractions weak and uncertain, and even, in some instances, producing marked irregularity of its rythm. A noticeable feature in such cases, is, that the most trifling causes will sometimes bring on violent attacks of palpitation; a few minutes of rapid walking; climbing several pairs of stairs hastily; the presence in the stomach of indigestible articles of food; any sudden mental excitement, even though trivial in its nature, and a variety of equally simple and unimportant causes, are often sufficient to provoke severe attacks of palpitation, which may also prove quite obstinate, "According to the experiments of Sir Benj. Brodie, tobacco causes paralysis of the heart, through the medium of the nerves "—and this conclusion gives additional importance to the facts above detailed in their relation to insurance. Mr. Lizars gives an account of an excessive smoker who was subject to terribly severe attacks of angina pectoris; after an unusually severe and prolonged attack, which came near proving fatal, he abandoned smoking altogether, and the disease disappeared without any treatment. Severe dyspepsia is a very frequent result of using tobacco, and is in general very obstinate when dependent upon this cause ; obstinate constipation is another of its evil results ; from these two evils result emaciation and general debility, laying the foundation for various nervous diseases. A disorder very much resembling delirium tremens was several times witnessed by the late Dr. Chapman, and by him attributed to this potent agent; the patients recovered on abandoning their pipes. In the reports of nearly every Insane Asylum in the United States, may be found several cases of insanity charged to the account of tobacco. In the form of snuff it sometimes becomes poisonous, on account of being contaminated with lead during the process of manufacture—thus producing lead colic or lead palsy. It would be easy to extend this list of symptoms to very much greater length, but sufficient has already been said to indicate its more general and prominent effects.

Does the use of tobacco tend, materially, to shorten life ? Candid, unprejudiced observations on this point are very much needed. As yet we have no data upon which to found an opinion—much less to base a statement of *facts*. Several American "Counterblasts" have been launched against this persecuted weed; each as valueless and impotent as that of the Royal fop of England ; the clergy, the press and the medical profession, have severally waged war against tobacco, and yet it remains and will remain the delight of millions.

There can be no doubt that an excessive use of tobacco—especially by a person of feeble constitution—does tend, materially, to shorten life. Moreover, a person whose blood is already poisoned by nicotine, is thereby rendered less capable of surviving severe attacks of acute diseases, and this is a proper matter for the examiner to consider. Severe and obstinate dyspepsia, angina pectoris, or oft-recurring palpitation—especially if they exist in persons excessively addicted to the use of tobacco—demand rejection. For, even if it cannot be clearly shown that tobacco is the underlying cause, its use most assuredly adds one more element of danger in the case, and one much more likely to remain permanently, than to be removed by a resolute effort on the part of the applicant.

INDEX.

A

	Page.
Artists	16
Artisans	16
Age	18, 73
Acclimation	25
Army Employment	28
Asthma	29, 83
Apoplexy	29, 131
Ancestors Longevity	56
Answers of Applicant	64
Appearance, General	69
Aspect of Countenance	70
Age, Apparent	73
Aphonia	83
Aneurism of Heart	101
Aneurisms	108
Angina Pectoris	101
Adhesions, Heart	101
Atrophy, Heart	101
Aortic Obstruction	105
Aortic Regurgitation	105
Abdominal Organs	109
Atrophy of Liver	112
Atrophy of Mucous Membrane	116
Albuminuria	119
Addison's Disease	123
Atrophy of Brain	133
Asthenia, Nervous	136
Abscesses	143
Amputations	54, 146

B

Bronchitis	31
Bones, Size of	81
Bilious Temperament	74
Blood Murmurs	107
Blood Vessels, Disease of	108
Bright's Disease	119
Brain, Disease of	130
Brain Chron. Poisoning	136
Blanks, Filling up of	150

C

	Page
Climate	25
Consumption	32
Cholic	32
Cardiac Diseases	33
Chorea	37
Catarrh	42
Cough, Habitual	53
Chest Measurement	67
Complexion	71
Color of Hair and Eyes	71
Congestion of Lungs	84
Cyanosis	102
Congestion, Liver	111
Cirrhosis of Liver	112
Calculus	122
Cystitis, Chronic	122
Cerebro-Nervous System	124
Convulsions	126
Co-ordination, Defective	127
Coup de Soliel	135
Cutaneous Affections	143
Climacteric, Female	145
Constitution	147
Cachexia	149
Certificates, Duplicates	151

D

Diseases, Previous	29
Dropsy	33
Diptheria	34
Dyspepsia	51
Dysentery	52
Diarrhœa	52, 114
Disease within Seven Years	55
Dyspnœa	85
Deposits, Pulmonary	85
Deposits, Signs of Pulmonary	86-88
Degenerations, Heart	102
Dilatation, Heart	102

INDEX.

	Page.
Degenerations, Liver	112
Digestion, Importance of	116
Diabetes	122
Duchenne's Disease	126
Deposits, Brain	133
Delirium Tremens	22, 137
Diathesis	148

E

Employment, Previous	29
Eyes	72
Emphysema	89
Empyæmia	91
Epilepsy	36, 126
Encephalitis	130

F

Fistula	34
Fits	36, 126
Friend, Reference to	62
Furunculi	143
Female Applicants	144

G

Gout	37
Gonorrhœa	49
Growths, Intracranial	133

H

Heart Disease	33, 93, 101
Hernia	43, 144
Hæmoptysis	46
Hæmatemesis	47
Hereditary Disease	18, 59, 138
Height	66
Hair	71
Hydrothorax	91
Heart—Signs of Disease:	
Location	94
Bulging or Depression	94
Impulse	94
Area of Dullness	95
Pulsation	96
Sounds	98
Location of Sounds	100
Non-organic Disease of	106
Hypertrophy, Heart	102
Hepatitis, Chronic	113
Hæmorrhoids	116
Hysteria	36, 126
Hypertrophy of Brain	133
Hip Disease	144

I

Intemperance	22, 136
Insanity	37, 130, 137
Injury, Traumatic	34

	Page.
Insurance, Previous	63
Identity of Applicant	65
Idiosyncrasy	76
Inspection	80
Intestinal Tube	114
Intellection, Derangement	130

J

Jaundice	39
Joints	144

K

Kidneys, Disease of	118
" Enlargement of	118

L

Life Expectation	19
Liver, Disease of	38, 111
Longevity of Ancestors	56

M

Mechanics	16
Marriage	20
Muscles, Contour of, etc	72
Mensuration	78
Movements, Respiratory	80
Malformations, Heart	103
Myocarditis	103
Mitral Regurgitation,	105
" Obstruction	105
Motion, Derangement of	125
Menstrual Functions	145
Metritis, etc	146

N

Name	15
Nervous Temperament	74
Neuralgia, Intercostal	92
Nutrition	117
Nephritis, Chronic	118
Nephralgia	118
Nervous Asthenia	136

O

Occupation	15
Opium Eating	23

P

Professional Men	16
Paralysis	40, 128, 142
Palpitation	40
Parents, Living or Dead, etc	58
Physician, Family	61
Phlegmatic Temperament	74
Pulse	76
Pneumothorax	91
Pleurodynia	91

INDEX.

	Page.
Pericarditis	103
Pancreas	113
Prostate, Enlarged	122
Poisoning of Brain	136
Pregnancy and Parturition	144
Phlegmasia Dolens	146

Q
Quinsy	40

R
Residence	15
Residence, Foreign	25
Rheumatism	41, 51
Rupture	43
Rejection, Previous	63
Respiratory Organs	78
Respiratory Organs, Diseases of	82
Rigidity of Muscles	128
Ramollissement, Brain	134
Ramollissement, Spinal Cord	142
Risk, General Character	147

S
Sobriety	21
Scarlatina	45
Spitting of Blood	46
Syphilis	49
Stricture	49, 122
Skin	71

	Page
Sanguine Temperament	73
Stomach	111
Spleen	114
Sensation, Derang. of	129
Spasms	126
Softening of Brain	134
Softening of Spinal Cord	142
Sunstroke	135
Spinal Diseases	141
Senses Special, Loss	144

T
Temperance	21
Temperament	73, 147
Tumors, Intrathoracic	92
Tremor	125
Tumors	144

U
Urinary Organs, Disease of	47
Ulcers	143

V
Vaccination	24
Valvular Changes, Heart	104
Varicose Veins	143

W
Weight	66

INDEX TO APPENDIX.

	Page.
Acclimation	162
Alcohol, Effects of	162
Applicants, Female	175
Brain, Softening of	173
Blood, Spitting of	167
Consumption	163
Clergyman's Sore Throat	154
Colored Races, Mortality of	160, 161
Diarrhœa, Camp	163
Females, Longevity of	176
Insanity	165
Intemperance	161
Inebriates, Safety of	162
Locomotor Ataxy	172
Labor, Mortality from	175

	Page.
Mortality, Tables of	157, 158
Mortality, from various Diseases	156
Nephralgia	165
Occupation, Effects of	151
Public Speakers, Safety of	154
Professional Men	154
Physicians	154
Puerperal Fever, Mortality from	176
Palpitation	166
Pulse	171
Sexes, Mortality of	159
Teachers	154
Tobacco, Effects of	176
Urine, Examination of	169
Vertigo	173

www.ingramcontent.com/pod-product-compliance
Lightning Source LLC
Chambersburg PA
CBHW020250170426
43202CB00008B/298